Pages
Part 1: THE WAR YEARS Recollections of Childhood	2 to 42
Part 2: PROFILE OF GREAT TEW A Brief History	44 to 46
Part 3: A 1000 YEARS OF HISTORY	48 to 71

Preface

My motive for writing this book is to place on record the life of the village at a certain time in its history before it is lost forever. It is written with pure love and affection for the people who lived there during the last war some of whom still live there to-day. The impression made on a casual visitor or sight-seer would be purely superficial. To understand the way of life and outlook one would have to live there. For that reason it had to be written. It will not be welcomed by those who take exception to the intrusion into their lives. Any book of a personal nature will be regarded as an invasion of privacy and be, possibly, contentious.

I have endeavoured to be as accurate as possible and not set out to offend. By using situations, mostly connected with my own behaviour, I have hopefully succeeded in giving character to the people involved and the places of interest. The village is seen through my eyes. I have not deliberately invented anything or exaggerated for effect. Neither have I dwelt on the hard times which they were undoubtedly during the war. These are the recollections of childhood fondly remembered and should be regarded as such. I would not wish to change any part of them as they were the happiest time in our lives as a family within a community of village people and an experience not to be missed.

Grove Ash Farm
Great Sew,
Oxon
28-2-91

Dear Michael,
How nice it was to hear from you after all these years, but I am sorry you still bear such a grudge after such a long time, I know we shared many happy times together.

That is why I'm sorry I will not add any information to your manuscript as so much of it is untrue and a figment of your imagination. it is an insult to the people who lived at Great Sew during those difficult times, you write about families having very little money and children running about with no clothes, surely you must have known that a mans wage for a weeks work at that time was £1-7-6p not much to clothe and bring up a family. as there were no state handouts either.

This sort of story is not a true reflection on our way of life. as long as you have health and happiness what more can you ask for. Once again I am sorry that you can only remember the worst times of your stay at Great Sew.

Yours sincerely, Tony.

The Green and The Post Office.

The Post Office and Falkland Arms.

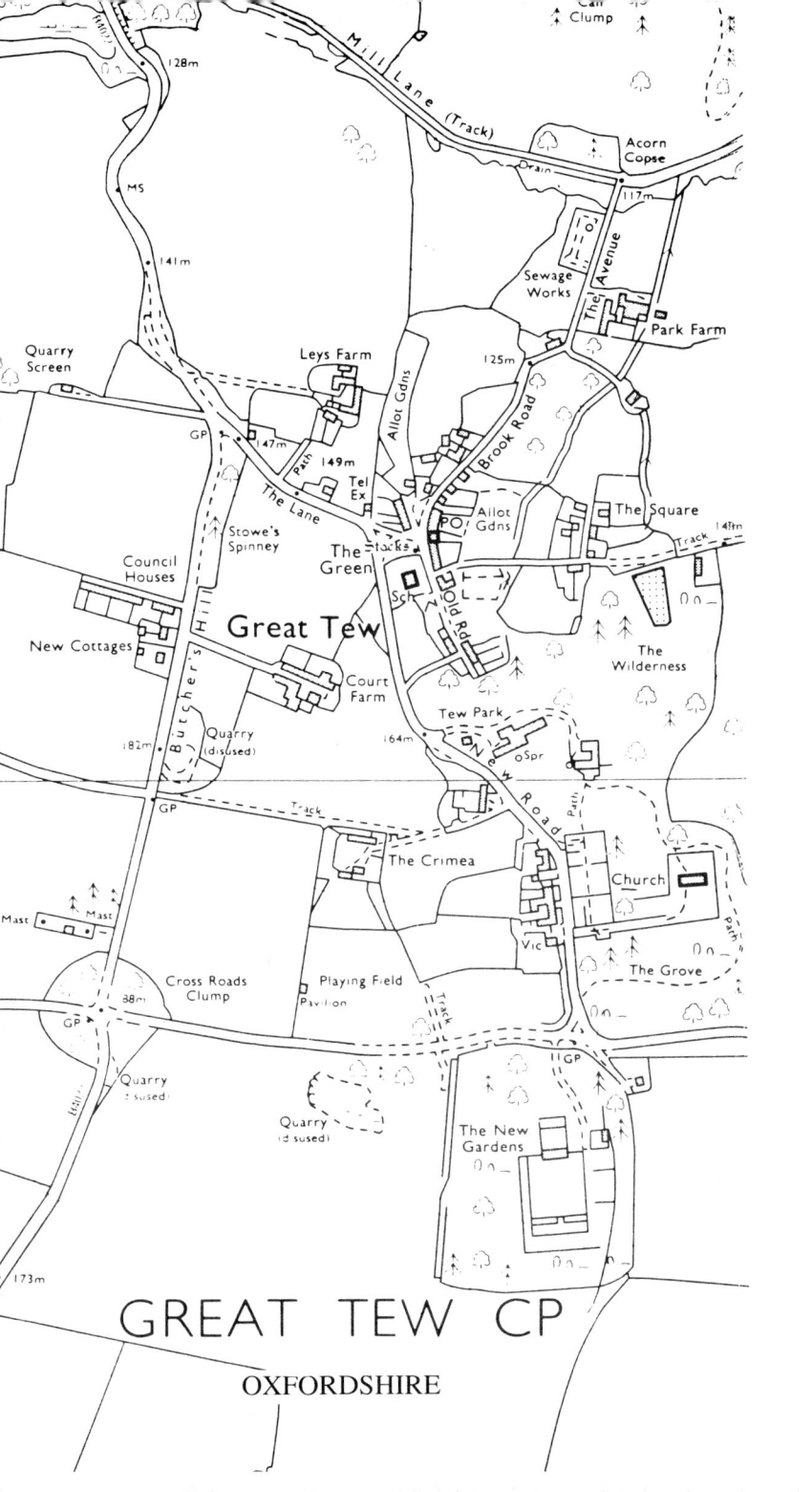

A Place Of Pilgrimage

Chapter 1

I don't remember the precise moment we arrived at the village. We were all too young having just started school. It was sometime in September 1939 just after the declaration of war against Germany. We were evacuees but on reflection probably refugees in our own country. We, the second wave of Varneys had arrived from Ealing, West London on the advice of Grandma Fisher to join a rather elderly Aunt 'Jinny', her sister, who lived in the village two-doors down the slope from the Post Office.

There we were Mrs.Vera Varney, son Raymond, son Michael (me) and daughter Maureen. At that time we three children were between 4 and 7 years of age. Father Sydney had been sent to Bath by the Admiralty to play his part in the war effort and was not to be seen much thereafter. We were to be occupied in plenty. I remember being happy and excited like all children on an adventure who had just arrived in a removal van with our bare essentials outside the Falkland Arms. We, with the other Varneys, Brian and John, our cousins on fathers side, were to occupy the village for 5 years. It was an invasion which left its mark for a generation.

We as a family were to stay with Aunty Lil and Uncle Charlie, Brian and John in their thatched cottage on the Old Road alongside the village green for a time until we could find somewhere else to live. I remember the cold uneven stone-flagged floors, the narrow staircase by the front door leading to the bedrooms one of which overlapped next doors'; all very reminiscent of the nursery rhyme 'The Three Bears'. It was very cramped with Aunty Lil ruling the roost over five unruly children. We were to go out and stay out. My mother and Aunty Lil were not to be the best of friends being very protective towards their respective children. Uncle Charlie spent all his time cycling away to work beyond Bicester 22 miles away as there was little work to do in the village except at harvest time.

Great Tew, reputedly the prettiest village in Oxfordshire, together with Duns Tew and Little Tew, were first mentioned in the Domesday Book of 1086. From its earliest recorded ecclesiastical origins in 990 AD Great Tew's history evolved through Norman ownership to being partitioned and unified in 1536. At the end of the 16th century Tew Park was created and much of the present village was built immediately after Lord Falkland met his fate at the Battle of Newbury in 1643 and during two building phases between 1816-18 and 1850-56 when the road system and plan of the village took its final shape.

Through the centuries the village had been in some kind of time warp. Its character was distinctly medieval and seemingly unchanged by the passage of time. Isolated with no electricity, no gas, no mains water, no sewerage but with 3 telephones in the whole village. All roads bypassed the village and took you to Oxford, Banbury or Chipping Norton. No one passed through. Locally, there was Enstone with Worths bus garage and the mighty bomber base, Ledwell with its pit and Little Tew which was wryly said to be bigger than Great Tew and which was just past the crossroads over the hill. The villagers talked about the Great Rollright stones, the weekly visit to 'Chippy', the fortnightly visit to Banbury, the once-a-month shopping trip to Oxford and the Varneys. Rationing had been introduced and peace was at an end.

For its part in the war effort Great Tew had its stocks threatening its presence on The Green for all to see between the school, the pub and the horse trough. It had served a primitive purpose but now provided a toy for the children and their mischief. Likewise the horse trough had little use except on fox-hunt days and for children who were forbidden to play in it just in case a passing animal needed a clean drink.

The village school stood in solid Cotswold stone ready to receive its pupils should they attend. The pub named after Lucius Cary, Viscount Falkland, looked up to the school and the Manor House. Apart from the Village Hall, some way away towards the Banbury Road, the pub was the centre of life in the village. It occupied a central point between the three greens to attract custom and it did so mostly at night when the farming community ended their day.

Not far away stood the 'spreading chestnut tree', resplendent in the middle of the green by the Old Road. It could easily have inspired the words for the song as it embraced its surroundings. The cluster of cottages was all that was needed to set the scene for a pastoral setting. Down the road from the pub opposite the horse trough was the Post Office selling groceries and provisions to save the trip to town. Further down on the next green by the well almost tucked away in the opposite corner was 'Aunt' Ada's Shop selling sweets, haberdashery and fireworks when the time was right. The thatched cottages on three sides almost enclosed the green with the row of laurel bushes hiding the 2 cottages at one end. It was a sight full of rustic charm whichever way one looked.

At the side of the pub ran a lane down a hill and up the other side to 'The

Square' which loosely described the scattered cottages with thatched roofs spread across the brow of the hill. Beyond them in the wooded grounds of the Manor House was the 'Wilderness'. A forbidding place except for children looking for adventure.

On the hill in its own grounds overlooking the village and connected by a dark path and an iron swing gate stood the Manor House with its own drive higher up and wrought iron gates leading to the main road. It stood majestically dominating the village and the villagers below as it had done for centuries past. It was lord and master of all it surveyed. The villagers knew their true place. They remained subservient until they went to the Norman Church, St. Michael's, further up the hill past the Blacksmiths when they were then above the Manor House. Also on higher ground above the village, the villagers had thought to place their cricket pitch midway between the Church and the crossroads but not out of bounds.

Even in those days there was a telephone box opposite the school hidden away in the corner of The Green. There was no running water apart from the streams at the very bottom of the village. Water was available in wells scattered around the village often shared by several households. In an emergency there was always the 'Wilderness'.

All around the village were the farms mostly for grazing dairy herds. They were as one, a tight community living with and for each other not welcoming to outsiders. Some of the people had never left the village. The villagers were reclusive at times diffident but self-sufficient.

Looking down Brook Road.

Inside Out

Chapter 2

Our arrival in the village meant the end of peacetime for the villagers. If only they had known in advance what bad luck the Cruel Fates had cast in their direction for the next 5 years they would surely have banished us from the start. The Germans were at war with the British and the Varneys were at war with the Cliftons, the Tustains, the Lowes and the rest of the village or so it seemed at times. It was not a war of our choosing as we were escaping from the Nazis to the Cotswolds to Oxfordshire to rural England.

We, as children, were unaware of the conflict around us being sheltered in our innocence from the adult world and too young in our tender years to understand prejudice or innuendo. We were neither sensitive nor part of the social scene. It was every child's dream of pleasure and adventure. Only occasionally did we feel unwelcome when names began to fly. All children quarrel particularly when they are poles apart. That is when one repeats ones parents private or not so private opinions. We were called 'London Bug squashers' and they became 'Country Bumpkins'. They were not words that we could possibly invent. The words fitted the need for insult. Parents fell out for weeks and children fell out for days with the antagonism being fuelled by parents trying to avoid neighbours to keep the peace.

Apart from the two Varney families the war years saw the invasion of the village by the Lowes, the Pantins, the Marketus's and the Gibsons. Some of the villagers served in the war like Edgar Dolphin who spent most of it in a Prisoner of War Camp in Poland and Tom Clifton was with the 8th Army but Eric Lewell was not to survive the D-Day landing. Two other villagers also lost their lives in action including Rodney Coles.

Life in the village went on as it had always done in a quiet, peaceful way. Only on rare occasions was the peace broken as when, some time after we had settled in, I received a woeful head injury by being pushed against a gate post outside the Coles' House by Tony Clifton who will later feature quite prominently in this story. Seeing my mothers rage and hearing the tension in her voice Tony escaped being smacked on the backside and ran off home laughing to tell his mother. Not long after we had arrived home Mrs Clifton came to the cottage to shout her head off at the front door believing she was in the right whilst we listened out of harms way. My mother was left in no doubt of the consequences if she so much as laid a

The Varneys, Vera, Raymond, Michael and Rusty.

Brookside Cottage

Tony Clifton, Olive Panton, George Clifton and Mavis Clifton, August 1940.

hand on her child or even thought about it. The world was to blame and Tony of course.

Within weeks of our arrival, and not too soon for us all, we left Aunty Lil and Uncle Charlie and moved to the bottom of the village to Brookside Cottage which belonged to the farmer, Mr Tustain, who reluctantly let us stay there. As we arrived in the removal van there was a reception committee of children to look at us. The cottage was isolated with a stream running down the side outside the garden and was attached at right angles to the only other house occupied by Sid and May Crook. In the 17th century it was a bakers and flour mill but had later been walled up to make two separate units to accommodate farm workers. We had been cast away or providence had lent a hand in placing us next door to the Crook family and their son 'Crackers' Crook who was our own age. It was here also that Aunty Margaret came to live with her brother-in-law Sid Crook whilst her husband Bill, the other son of Aunt 'Jinny', was away from it all fighting a real war somewhere in North Africa. Aunty Margaret, who blinked her way through life, worked at the Manor House which was later to be filled with the handicapped children, some orphaned as a result of bombing raids, from a school in Croydon.

Brookside Cottage had no mains water, no electricity and no toilet except at the very bottom of the garden like the rest of the village. Water came by hand in a bucket from a well next door in the garden belonging to the Crooks. The well was shared by frogs, snails and children when nobody was looking. We were often caught out by Aunty May who was short on temper and shorter on speed. When we were not lost in the vastness of the countryside we were chasing her chickens round the garden or in her chicken run. Mrs Crook's hobby so it seemed was collecting nails for her husband and chickens from their perambulations. A great deal of our time seemed to have been spent banging nails into every available plank of wood.

Our garden was bare and overgrown apart from a withering old apple tree in one corner that struggled to bear fruit and a damson tree in the other corner leaning over an old pigsty with the toilet attached. This stone relic served no other purpose than as a climbing frame with its cladding of ivy. The apple tree served the same purpose. The only feature of the garden apart from the occasionally worked vegetable patch was the rockery my father built, as was his obsession, at the side of the cottage. The long path to next door was bordered by the hedge which hid the garden from view and the stream which was crossed by a wooden bridge at the end of the garden. The two streams met under the bridge and formed the two boundaries.

Much of our play time was spent in the water getting wet, dirty and racing 'boats' of every description. A particular favourite was puncture-outfit chalk tins provided courtesy of the war. It was behind the hedge out of sight of the rest of the world that Raymond and I conceived our most wicked behaviour. On one cruel occasion we hung up the cat 'Rusty' on the washing line by its front paws. Swinging backwards and forwards the poor cat was unable to get off and hung on for dear life. The countryside was full of hazards for cats going about their business and not related to childish behaviour. There was the time when 'Rusty' came home with a 3 inch tear in its hind leg and had to be nursed back to health. Later the poor cat narrowly escaped death by coming home after 5 days with a wire noose round its neck, bound so tight that it had difficulty in breathing. She was probably saved by somebody cutting her free. Much later she had to be put down and although our mother managed to 'dispose' of unwanted kittens she was not disposed to dealing with a full grown cat and Bill Clifton had to be called in with his gun. It was shot out of our sight and buried secretly in the garden as we were too upset. Our concern for the cat was so overwhelming that we dug it up and I lifted it by the tail to check it was dead.

The cottage itself had been converted for farmhands who were more used to the cold and damp. A fire in the living room grate was needed for heat and for cooking. The uneven stone floor chilled the feet in the morning and made pools of water from the copper boiler in the scullery on Monday washday when the cottage filled with steam, smoke and sweat. It was gruelling work for our mother. Clothes-line pegs were at a premium and made convenient toys for ill-clad dirty children. The chimneys themselves were vast as caverns and needed sweeping regularly by the village sweep to prevent chimney fires which when they happened could be dangerous.

We were as comfortable as could be expected with our meagre, albeit upholstered furniture from London. Certainly the rats and mice were more comfortable than we were. At night we could hear them running around inside the walls which in the dark was a terrifying experience. I can remember when Raymond was away in London and sister Maureen had been taken into mothers bed because she was frightened, sleeping by myself in the back bedroom screaming my head off for hours under the covers imagining the clock moving round the room by someone's hand and the rats being on the shelf looking for candles to chew above the chimney breast. My cries for 'Mum' to let me sleep in her bed with sister Maureen were to no avail and I felt very alone and victimised. That cured me, as I was never afraid of the dark again. As for 'Rusty' the cat she shared the larder cupboard with the mice and spent more time having kittens than catching mice. The mice seemed to know what mouse-traps were for and the rats what day of the week it was. At night we used to steal down the narrow twisting stairs to catch out the cockroaches before they ran for their hiding places. We expected to find them carpeting the floor from the tales we had heard but never did.

At the end of the leafy lane leading from Brookside stood two magnificent copper beeches which grew at the bottom of Morleys orchard. Many hours were spent up one of these trees by all the children noisily singing their heads off towards the cottages. These cottages, reposed on the other side of the road at the corner of the bend and were occupied by the Lowe's and the Cliftons. Tustains Farm (Park Farm) was just around the corner with the farmhouse standing back proudly from the quiet of the lane leading down to Coles's Brook and from there up to Cow Hill. Here was a community all by itself with the children mixing with one another but not the parents and certainly not the Tustains who only came out of hiding when a cow escaped or it was harvest time or when Mr Tustain was after my blood.

Brook Road Cottages.

The Cliftons and Lowes faced different ways in life. Bill Clifton was a farm hand and very much a man of the soil working to all hours and coming home to farm his family and garden after work. It was no wonder he was small in build and big in humour. His wife, Gert, was a big rounded woman bursting out of her clothes with laughter most of the time. In between feeding the chickens and pigs she would be feeding her four children. George was the eldest too young for a mans job but not too old to be chasing 5 year old sister Maureen around for kisses. Tony the second son was his mothers favourite and sought her protection whenever friendships broke down. Mavis the eldest daughter was just what father ordered as a little girl. Later on Gillian arrived amongst much commotion with high expectations dashed by being handicapped with a foot back to front. After many operations in the Ratcliffe Infirmary, Oxford her leg did get straightened out but she always seemed to be hobbling around in plaster, trying to catch up. She was a depressing child with a limp to match. The Cliftons were in every respect a down to earth family, a farming family, surviving on the produce of their own labours and a take home pay of £1.7s.6p a week. There were no state handouts to help make ends meet.

As for the Lowes, there was Mrs Lowe and her two sons John and Michael. Mrs. Lowe was divorced and had arrived at the cottage six months earlier. Her two boys were totally different in nature and appearance. Michael was fair and pure skinned whilst John suffered from exema which made his skin flake off every time he scratched himself which he did constantly. Their mother, a Quaker and a principled woman, with no sign ever of a smile on her face refused to have her children immunised against diptheria and paid the price by losing Michael. We stood and looked at Michael's bedroom window wondering how such a thing could happen. Mrs.Lowe was then left with John whom she immediately had immunised but it was no cure for his skin complaint.

Mrs Lowe kept a flower garden and kept her hedges trimmed but that was all. Next door at the Cliftons the garden was much more functional. The chickens seemed to rule the roost with a large area wired off and pecked clean with their foraging. For some historical reason the middle of the garden had been chosen as the final resting place for the remains and tomb of Lord Falkland as well as for the garden tools. It was a mile away from the Norman Church at the top of the village but served as a convenient perch for any chicken who could reach it with clipped wings. At the back of the house was the obligatory pigsty always occupied by the most enormous beast being fattened for ritual slaughter. On one occasion we witnessed with some kind of fascination the slaughter of a pig after its throat had been cut and its deafening squeals died away with its blood and life. We three children had to watch from a hump outside the garden as we were suffering in our own way with measles and the other children would not come near us. The carcus when cleaned up with the bristles burnt was cured and hung for provisions until the next pig was ready.

Early on at Brookside a London girl named Barbara Allen who was much our own age came to be billeted with us. She was a quiet girl with just her father John to look after her. We were horrible to her because she was a Roman Catholic. We teased her about not having a mother and would not let her play with our toys of which there were precious few. The other girls were equally cruel by running off and leaving her. Some time later she went to live with the Gibbards, the blacksmiths, by the Vicarage. On one of his visits, her father met Aunty Margarets friend, Doreen, proposed and married her after Barbara had made friends by chasing the bride-to-be around the garden trying to put a worm down her neck with father joining in the fun.

Away from the haven of the village, past Tustains farm, stretched an expanse of countryside to be explored. The bridge over Coles's Brook was as inviting as the brook itself. When the water was low we spent our playtime under the bridge and in the mud of the stream above and below the watercress beds and when the floods came we stood on the bridge and watched the water reach halfway up the fields with a torrent in the middle flooding the road. Beyond the lane to left and right stood Cow Hill dotted with cows and trees. The lane to the left led to Mrs. Marquetus's and to the right miles away was to be found the derelict Watermill, Betteridges Farm (Cottenham Farm), the bluebell woods and the Brains.

The Brain family was related directly to the Cliftons. Mr Brain was the weediest man you could ever meet. Yet his wife was one of the largest women in the area. Between them they had managed, if that is the right word, to produce nineteen children in fewer years. All the children ran around snotty-nosed, dirty and ill-clad. Mavis their cousin would often take clothes over to them and we were all given a big welcome. The parents could not say 'no' to the joys of life. Despite the apparent happiness there were moments of tragedy when one of the children was murdered and the twentieth child died. You had the feeling that they had somehow worn themselves out.

Nature In The Raw

Chapter 3

Just three miles away from Tew was Enstone. In more ways than one it was our lifeline. Not only was it a Bomber Base on the hill between the two villages but also provided a link with the world around us through Worths Bus Garage to Chipping Norton, Banbury and Oxford. It consisted of a shack, a pump for rationed petrol and a couple of antiquated buses with wooden seats. Apart from the weekday bus to the secondary school at 'Chippy' the less frequent buses to Banbury or Oxford were anticipated with some excitement by the ladies in the village for their shopping trips. Not that there was much money to spend. It was an escape and a chance to go window shopping or to go to one of the two cinemas.

Not long after we had arrived in the village an event occurred which was to transform many people's lives and remain in our memories and evoke our feelings forever. One summer morning in 1941 the bus arrived to wait at the top of The Green by the gate to Louches Farm for the weekly shopping trip to 'Chippy'. We children went to wave goodbye to our mothers through the windows of the bus. The usual high-spirits of the occasion were to come to a sudden and tragic end. Down the hill came a car to pass the stationary bus on the other side of the road. At that moment Tony Clifton ran round the back of the bus to look for his mother and was swept away by the car. He was carried twenty yards down the hill as the van veered to the right trapped underneath with only the gravel between him and the road. Screams filled the air amidst the pandemonium. Tony was still pinned underneath the car when his mother arrived. She was expecting her fourth child Gilly and had run in great haste to rescue Tony. Both children were to suffer as a result. Tony with a badly scarred eye and face and Gilly with a twisted foot. Years later both were to have surgery to correct their defects.

When Autumn arrived each year there was feverish excitement outside the Falkland Arms as the hounds and huntsmen gathered to go on a foxhunt. We children stood and watched the dogs in their pack and the men on horseback in their red. It all seemed very calm until they set off and then the pace quickened by degrees. We ran miles across the fields to keep up. They only paused when a fox was trapped and the hounds became even more excited. One day down at the old watermill a fox had been cornered in the old workings and the baying of the hounds gave it away. It would not come out except with much persuasion to be pounced upon by the hounds who tore it apart and the huntsman who was quick enough to cut off its brush as a trophy. When foxes met their end by gunshot or trap the whole fox skin was hung, dried and lined as a much sought-after wrap for the ladies. It was held in place with a clip fixed under the chin of the fox to snap it fast onto the tail.

In our wanderings around the countryside we soon became aware of rabbits and rooks. Just about everybody connected or not with farming had one or more sixteen-bore shotguns racked up in the hall or living room. There were traps everywhere. Wire nooses along the runs and metal sprung traps in the entrances to holes not to mention the ferrets kept for hunting in garden cages. The men went out at random, according to their allotted areas, to catch them, bringing them back tied together by their legs lying across the front and back of their shoulders. There was never enough to go round to supplement rationed meat and the catch was sold or claimed very quickly. We all had to become efficient at skinning rabbits as well as plucking chickens to keep ourselves fed.

Even I, so young, enjoyed the thrill of owning my own ferret which was bought at the great cost of five shillings from a farm miles away on the way to Banbury. I had a sack to carry it in and a pair of leather gloves to handle it with. It was kept in a cage in the pigsty away from the house. The animal would attack me with its sharp penetrating teeth whenever I fed it and yet I still treated it like a pet. One day we went ferreting with it across the back fields on Tustains land past the 'Faraway Tree' and put it down a suitable burrow with a collar round its neck and a cord attached. My pet ferret had taken about four paces towards the hole on its first outing and from beneath the ground snapped a trap clamping the poor animals front leg between its teeth. It needed all our strength to prise the jaws apart and to hold back the tears from our tragic experience. The ferret limped around in its cage day after day under our care and became so tame after a time that we could pick it up and stroke it like a real pet. It had learnt a painful lesson on how to behave.

On another outing with the ferret we decided to go rabbiting in the fields by Banbury Hill which was a long way from home. We were told ferreting was illegal as farmers and farmhands had areas reserved for them but it made no difference to us pursuing our interest. The first rabbit we caught after digging out the hole just lay there in fear of the ferret. I picked it up by the hind legs and wacked it with the back of my hand on the back of its neck to kill it following the example of my elders. I put the stunned rabbit down and it disappointingly ran off across the field. Undeterred we went further afield to another warren to let the ferret go. That was our undoing as the noose slipped from around its neck when pulled to retrieve it and the ferret stayed down the burrow. We three spent hours digging in the ground for 'our' ferret and night fell on the long summer evening. Our mother had spent hours searching the countryside for us and eventually came across us in the dark. We had lost track of time and she had found us in tears with some relief. What happened to the ferret we never knew.

The rooks were a different matter altogether one could never catch them in the trees or on their nests very easily. Their rookeries were well known to the villagers well away in isolated clumps of trees at such places as the Crossroads between the two Tews. Parties of men each carrying a gun and a belt of ammunition would quietly approach the cross roads, stand under the trees to allow the birds to settle and all together open fire. Not many birds met their fate due to the height of the trees but it did provide pleasure and served as some kind of warning to the rooks under protest not to steal crops.

Floods and heavy snow interrupted our lives frequently and the pace of life slowed even more in the village making movement difficult. The flood waters were enjoyed in summer as warm pools were left in the fields to swim and play in. The snow covered the hillsides in winter and excursions were made to sledge down Cow Hill, down the hills above the village green and of course above Brookside in the field below Morleys Cottage. A real sledge was a prize possession and most had to be made by hand with strips of metal nailed on for runners. Children with absent fathers had to make do. The most popular vehicle was a tray or piece of bent metal from a farm. There were plenty of hazards to negotiate particularly molehills which being in abundance threw you up into the air without hope of recovery. Often when it was really cold the road above the village school served as long slides fifty or more feet in length. Some of our slides were a danger to local life such as the one we created at the top of The Cut. Miss Akers and Mrs Slatter who lived at the bottom of the hill were soon to complain as they could not then get up the steep hill to the top road.

Not all our outdoor activities took place during the day. We always knew when Aunty Margaret and our mother would be out playing cards or visiting for the evening. They did not tell us but we knew they often came home after mid-night so we never got caught. In our pyjamas, barefooted in the dead of night, we would steal out of the house and go as far away as

Coles's Brook a half mile away to try and catch a duck sitting on its nest. It seemed a good idea at the time as we had been told by George and Tony that it was there. We never found a thing and returned home none the worse for wear.

It was on the same patch of ground alongside Coles's Brook that we all had our first so to speak sexual experience. It happened in broad daylight in sight of the two lanes. Everyone seemed willing to play at the time with the boys being more persuasive. So the four girls with some reluctance lined up by the stream to play 'dicks'. All the boys had one more or less when they dropped their trousers so with the girls partially clad we boys walked down the line poking the girls. Not all the girls showed the same interest in the game but did their best to join in the fun. Life became a little more promiscuous for us after that as we had by such means been initiated into 'country' ways if any encouragement were needed. We had it seemed been living a sheltered life in London as within two weeks of our arrival at Tew we knew the boys who were circumcised and those who were not. It made a difference to the girls. One soon learned that unless one was 'clean' so to speak 'haymaking' with all its pleasures was inconceivable. It was a fact of life not to be dismissed lightly.

We were surrounded by other temptations such as orchards on both sides of our lane. Much of our mischief was spent scrumping until we were frightened off by someone shouting at us from the other end of the orchard. Not all of our time was unproductive as I had a regular job working for Mr Tustain for a mere six old pence for the whole weekend. I worked very hard for that and had to be told to go home as I liked it too much and I was probably in the way. I just followed Mr Tustain around awaiting orders turning my hand to any dirty job. The real pleasure came in a trip to another farm or at harvesting when the machines such as they were went round the field in decreasing circles with farmhands waiting with guns raised to shoot the rabbits as they dashed for cover across the open field or to the nearest stooks.

A distraction to all this was the 'Faraway Tree' which stood in a field behind the house. Despite the grazing cows a long branch had survived at a level just above the ground and was broad enough to climb onto as a swing which went up and down as you sat on it. Somehow it had possessed some kind of compelling magic for us children. It beckoned, so we came. We climbed onto and into it for protection. We were at one with nature as if living within our own family tree.

Not far away on the road to Enstone a different world was unfolding.

The Bomber Base was all activity having come into service in late 1940. The noise of the bombers, mainly Wellington 2's and Whitley 5's, taking off and flying over filled the air with sound and interest. We walked to the Base to watch the bombers taxying around the airfield and coming to rest a few yards away with no thought that we were spies. The area had been cleared of trees apart from where the road fell below the top of the hill. It was along this road that we walked to meet our father who had walked many times in the opposite direction from Worths Bus Garage. We always ran the last few hundred yards to greet him when he came into sight. The family was now complete for a little while before his return to Bath and the Admiralty.

Incidental Behaviour

Chapter 4

Hear ye! Hear ye! If there had been a Crier for all the misdemeanours in the village I would have been a suitable person to appoint had I have known what I was doing or come to that any one of us youngsters. Things just happened. There was no malicious intent. At the time it was mostly innocent pleasure. Boys will be boys and girls will be girls, well, so they say.

It was not helpful from a behavioural point of view having 'Crackers' Crook living next door and he being our best friend. We all encouraged one another and thought no more about it. Whole days were spent away from the house and his mother, May Crook, could be heard for miles around calling 'Crackers' home by bellowing " Michael!", "Michael!", in a voice which started low on the first syllable and ended up ten seconds later on a high prolonged second syllable. It served its purpose when she had faced in four different directions to make her calls.

Having joined the men with their guns on many occasions it was natural that we should want to emulate them. One day when May Crook was otherwise occupied we took it upon ourselves to borrow Sid Crooks sixteen-bore shotgun and went off across the fields to shoot our prey. It was as well that we had not taken a bigger gun for that would have broken a shoulder or two. As it turned out no real harm was done and a robin that I had tried to shoot at four paces was missed completely. At the end of the day 'Crackers' was found out and received a severe beating from his mother whilst we got off scot-free and avoided Mrs. Crook for several days for the sake of our health.

The heavy country air, the damp, the water and the muck were not conducive to good health. You survived by chance as there were many viruses ready to find victims. Brother Raymond was in all the filth and his manner invited Bill Clifton jokingly to give him two nicknames 'Professor' and 'Rake' which fitted him admirably. 'Rake' soon picked up the vernacular as if he had always lived in Tew and amused everyone with his "Ooh Aaaaah's" his "Our Old Kid" and "Kiddo" when he was referring to me, his brother and "Muck Spreddin" all to the point of fixation. 'Rake' saw no evil and thought no evil. He never thought for one moment of the consequences of his lack of hygiene. We three children had to take it in turns, a week at a time, to collect the milk from the Louch Farm (Court Farm) or the other Tustain Farm (Leys Farm) at the top of the village. It was quite a distance to walk every day. Raymond collected snails and had no means of carrying them home so what did he do? He carried them home by floating them in the milk so he told us some time later when it was too late. It is no wonder with his habits that he was the only one in the village who caught scabies.

Sister Maureen did not escape the rigours of the countryside as she had the unpleasant experience of catching ringworm, usually confined to cows not to humans. She had a outbreak on her scalp and another one on her behind where she had presumably sat on it and then transferred it to her head. It was treated with iodine but was quite persistent as were the screams from Maureen. On another occasion she was found to have lice living in her hair and had to sit at the table whilst mother combed them out on a piece of paper to be wrapped and taken to school the next day. The incident had to be reported and Monica Clifton was blamed. Both children were washed in an evil-smelling cleaner. For my part I was so to speak a little luckier as the only consequence of living in the country for five years was rheumatism and asthma. We all suffered from chilblains at some time; Raymond being the worst afflicted.

Down the lane by the side of the Falkland Arms was, as I said earlier, 'The Square' named presumably because of the layout of the cottages built there. On the right, on reaching the top of the hill set close to the lane was a long cottage occupied by the Pratts. Further on, past the Gibsons cottage on the corner, was the end of the lane marked by a farm gate open on the left and flanked on the right by a cotswold stone wall belonging to the Manor House. Over the wall was the most forbidding place imaginable. It was the 'Wilderness', an eerie gloomy habitat with a large pond partially filled with fallen trees and surrounded by overhanging branches from the woods beyond. The logs in the water were paths to walk on both slippery and dangerous. The clear pond water held an idle fascination for us all with frogs, tadpoles and newts swimming around in abundance. The behaviour of the frogs caused us some concern.They were trying to strangle each other from behind and we separated them with difficulty not knowing that they were fertilising their eggs at the time. The eggs were everywhere in clusters and in beads for the newts. No-one disturbed our playing. There was no need for a sign to tell people to keep out.

Just down the road from the Post Office and across the green from the Coleman's and the Coles' stood a terrace of cottages one of which was the home and shop of 'Aunt' Ada. She was an old lady before her time pale-faced with black hair shaped like a pudding basin with teeth that kept dropping down every time she opened her mouth to speak. We took pleasure harassing her all at once when we were buying things.

In her shop she sold sweets, elastic, pins, gob-stoppers, liquorice and on firework night; sparklers. The 5th November, 1940 was to be her ruin. I had been challenged by Tony Clifton and told by Freddy Asprin to throw a sparkler over the roof of Ada's Shop which I said was easy. The sparkler went up and up into the air and landed near to the top of the thatched roof. It continued to sparkle and soon the roof was on fire. Ada came out in a panic but there was nothing she nor anyone else could do except curse and run round in circles. The flames soon spread through the thatch threatening the whole roof and the roof next door. Tony blamed me when grown-ups enquired who by then had arrived in numbers. By the time the fire brigade arrived the whole roof was ablaze with flames twenty feet above the cottages. The four or so fire engines had come from miles around probably believing the whole village was on fire. The firemen unrolled their hoses firstly to the village pump and then, after that had failed, all the way to the 'Wilderness' but little water flowed as the distance and pressure up hill was against them. Poor mother was frightened. We were sent home as we were in the way and as darkness fell. The next day revealed a blackened hole where the shop once stood with burnt timbers on the floor and the adjoining cottage a half-burned wreck. The next day a policeman visited the school to speak to the whole school and later called at Brookside to speak to me in grave tones, his dark shape towering above me, saying that if I had been a little older I would have been sent to prison.

Not long after that incident our mother was away shopping in Banbury. At home by ourselves we lit a fire and a spark shot out and landed on the arm of an easy chair by the hearth. Unnoticed it began to smoke and burn inside the arm as it was stuffed with straw. The room filled with smoke as the chair continued to smoulder. Putting a fire out in a chair is a difficult operation especially when one fears what parents will do as punishment. The only way we discovered was to pour water down the arm when the chair was put on its back. Mother was not at all pleased when she came home but gave us the benefit of the doubt.

Some time later early one evening there was a loud crackling sound and a light that lit up the whole sky. We walked over the fields by the butchers to discover that the Village Hall along The Lane by the other Tustain's farm was on fire. The first thought that crossed villagers minds was where was

Michael Varney? The truth was that the accident had been caused by a parafin lamp which exploded when lit by Dora Clifton who was the caretaker and who had gone there to get things ready for the next day and got burnt for her trouble. Afterwards, all that remained was the brick base and the suspicion that perhaps after all I was really to blame.

Fire was a hazard of the countryside during harvesting and haymaking. Luckily there were no fires to contend with except man-made or boy-made ones. Our neighbour Mr. Tustain would often build a hayrick on the hill well behind us in sight of his farm. Being close at hand we found it convenient as a slide and a place to make a home whilst looking for mice. Quite close to his rick stood a water cylinder on wheels which on occasions was empty. Just for pleasure we stuffed the cylinder with hay and lit it. There was no danger to the rick as it was some way away but Mr Tustain thought his rick was on fire as it was in a direct line and raced up the hill to put it out shouting all the way and chasing us off in different directions. We were in trouble again when we got home as Mr Tustain had already called to express his annoyance.

The trouble we caused then was only to be exceeded later by me when a real catastrophy struck Mr. Tustain. During our stay at Great Tew we had few if any toys to play with as we were pretty destructive and due naturally to shortages occasioned by the war. We made bows and arrows like George and Tony Clifton out of hazel wood when the saplings had not been cut down to layer hedgerows and made battle tanks with turrets sawn out of fencing posts with nails as guns. The tanks were pulled along behind a length of string over the grass which was Raymonds way of making them look realistic.

Not to be outdone and having my own ideas of realistic looking tanks I uncoupled and stole the driving tracks of Mr.Tustain's combine harvester which he kept at the top of his farm in sheds by the 'Wilderness'. They made a good toy and took up the contours of the ground like a tank when dragged along behind. When Mr. Tustain came to use his combine some months later he discovered that a vital part was missing. He must have gone crazy with rage over the theft. Everybody in the village knew his misfortune in no time as news travelled fast. Eventually the thought struck him that I might be the culprit and he called at Brookside to discover them and to tell my mother I should be tanned. Her reply was that I had received more tannings than any boy in the village which seemed to satisfy him. The tracks were restored to their rightful owner and I was severely ticked off. I kept away from Mr. Tustain after that.

I could not be blamed for every accident particularly those caused by the airforce at Enstone. After bombing raids on Germany many struggled to get home and did not quite make it to the runway. On one occasion we, the whole family, had taken one bike to Enstone to say goodbye to father. We took it in turns to ride on the way back when out of the sky fell a plane which crashed into an adjoining field. We were told to stay put in the pitch black whilst mother pedalled off downhill to see if she could save the pilot. An hour later she returned saying the rescue services had arrived and avoided reporting on the fate of the pilot.

Some time later on a spot about midway between Little Tew and the new houses being built up Butchers Hill, where we played on occasions, a plane crashed in the corner of a field which could be heard for miles around. The airforce were quick to clear up the wreckage. We were banned from the site but did eventually reach the spot to dig up some relics to take home as souvenirs.

RESIDENTS 1939-45

1 Park Farm
Ralph Golby Tustain
Mrs Peggy Tustain
1 Roddy, 2 Colin,
3 Jennifer,
4 Katherine,
5 Daphne

2 Mrs Molly Lowe
1 John, 2 Michael

3 Bill Clifton
Mrs Gert Clifton
1 George, 2 Tony,
3 Mavis, 4 Gilly

4 Mrs Vera Varney
1 Raymond, 2
Michael, 3 Maureen

5 Sid Crook
Mrs May Crook
1 Michael,
Mrs Margaret Crook

6 Tulip Cottage
Ralph Tustain
Mrs Tustain

7 Mrs Wyton
Arthur Wyton
(Postman)

8 Mrs Marketus
1 Paul, 2 Michael,
3 Maureen

9 Fred Williams
Mrs Williams

10 Shop
Miss Aida Gregory

11 George Hooper
Mrs Martha Hooper

12 Teddy Brooks
Mrs Brooks

13 George White
Mrs Clara White

14 Fred Clifton
Mrs Dora Clifton
1 Peter, 2 Muriel,
3 Monica

15 Charles Keal
Mrs Annie Keal
1 Florence, 2 Julia,
3 Hubert, 4 James

16 Leys Farm
Jim Tustain
Oscar Tustain
Mrs Mary Tustain

17 Tom Pantin
Mrs Gladys Pantin
1 Olive, 2 Leonard,
3 John

18 William Morley
Mrs Rhoda Morley
1 Bill, 2 Dolly,
3 Jack

19 William Paintin
Mrs Paintin
1 Joan

20 Ralph Coleman
Mrs Lydia Coleman
1 Muriel, 2 Betty,
3 Pat

21 Richard French
Mrs French
1 Jack, 2 Joby, 3 Ron

22 Mrs Oscar Coles
1 Rodney, 2 Arthur,
3 Peggy

23 Mrs Jinny Crook

24 Post Office
Miss Chedzey
Miss Parrott

25 Ralph Clifton
Amy Clifton
George Clifton

26 Mrs Seaward

27 Mr Newell
Mrs Ruth Newell
1 Eric, 2 Ron

28 Falkland Arms
Alfred Davis
Mrs Eleanor Davis

29 Jack Keleher
Dorothy Keleher
Bill Keleher

30 Miss Townsend
Mrs Lindsey
Mrs Knibbs

31 Charlie Varney
Mrs Lil Varney
1 Brian, 2 John

32 Tommy Sirmon
Mrs Sirmon

33 Tom Kyle
Mrs Kate Kyle

34 Miss Akers

35 Bert Matthews
(Saddler and harness maker)
Mrs Matthews
1 John, 2 Michael,
3 David

36 Wilfred Slatter
(Estate carpenter)
Mrs Minnie Slatter
1 Betty, 2 Joan,
3 Rita

37 William Hitchcox
Mrs Hitchcox
1 Florrie, 2 Elsie,
3 Bill

38 Harry Monk
Mrs Elsie Monk
1 Walter, 2 Norman,
3 Peter, 4 Gladys

39 Horace Gibbard
Mrs Annie Gibbard

40 Court Farm
James Louch
Mrs Louch
1 Ellen, 2 John, 3 Mary

41 The Estate Office
J. Wilkins
Mrs Wilkins

42 Crimea Yard
Leonard Clifton
Mrs Elizabeth Clifton
1 Tom, 2 Ivor,
3 Eddie, 4 Ilia

43 William Clifton
Jack Clifton
Harry Clifton
Tom Clifton
Mrs Parsons

44 Charles Shelton
(Undertaker and wheelwright)

45 Fred Gibbard
Mrs Gibbard
1 Jack, 2 Horace,
3 Maud

46 Charles Attwood
Mrs Attwood
1 Percy

47 Blacksmiths
Jack Gibbard
Mrs Eva Gibbard

48 Mr Locke
Mrs Locke
1 Evelyn, 2 Christine,
3 John

49 Fred Newell
Mrs Newell
1 Derek

50 Vicarage
Rev. C. E. Salisbury

51 Tom Dolphin
Mrs Dolphin
1 Mary, 2 David,
3 Tom, 4 Louie,
5 Eva, 6 Edgar

52 Bert Pratt
Mrs Annie Pratt
1 Harold, 2 Stella,
3 Victor

53 Jim Gibson
Mrs Abigail Gibson
1 Elsie, 2 Gertie,
3 Violet

54 Charles Pratley
Mrs Pratley

55 Frank Reeves (Estate thatcher)
Mrs Reeves
1 Iris

56 Bert Morley
Mrs Nora Morley
1 Peter, 2 Alan

57 Joe Townsend
Mrs Sarah Townsend
1 Frank, 2 Bill,
3 Walter

58 Johnny Gough
Mrs Gough

59 William Woodford
Mrs Woodford

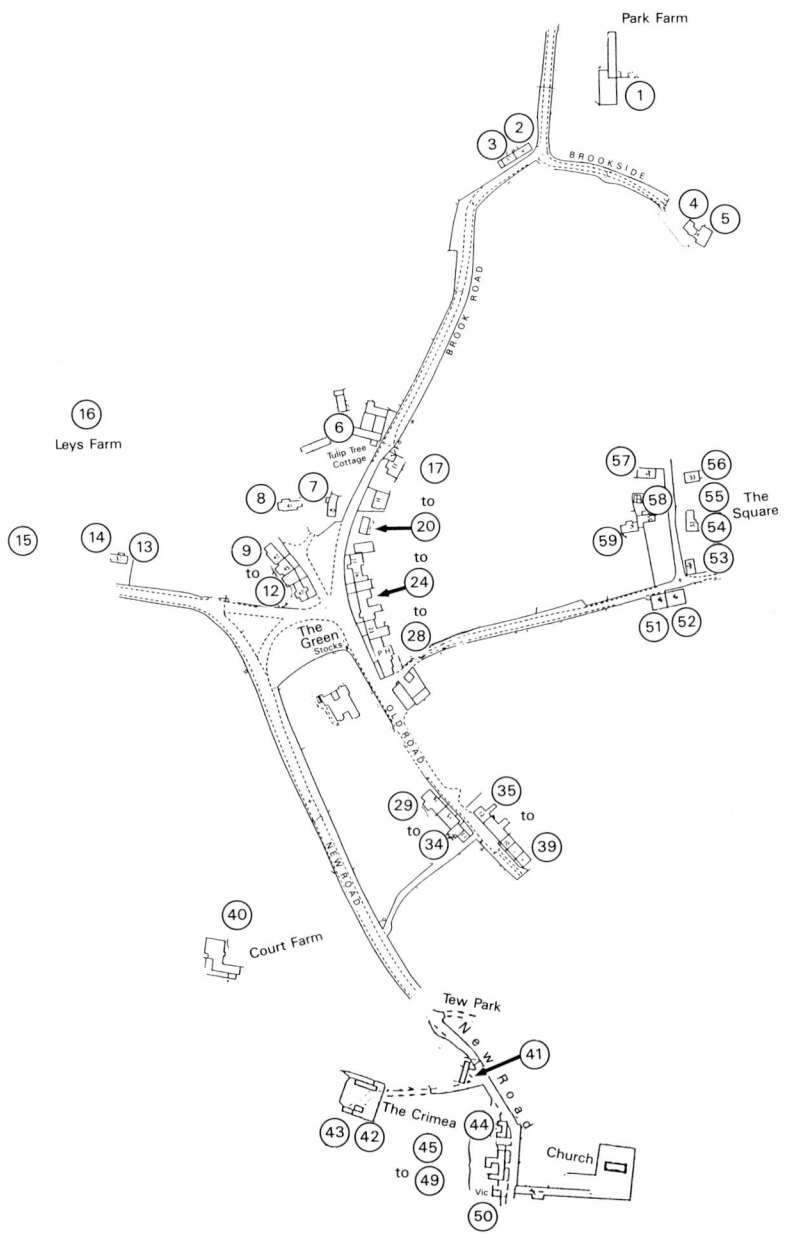

Back To Nature

Chapter 5

The Land Army was a necessary resource of wartime. As the men were taken off to serve in the forces the women volunteered to work on the land. There were few women farm workers until the war came to change working practices and attitudes. The women were easily distinguished by their brown outfits and trousers. They lived on the farms and worked on the farms hardly venturing beyond their boundaries. Initially their duties were confined to the care of livestock but extended as their experience grew to driving tractors and the other heavier needs of agriculture.

When the moment arrived for harvesting, for picking mangold wurzels for cattle or for 'spud picking' it was all hands to the plough. The harvest came first and was duly rewarded at 3 pence an hour to ensure it was all brought in on time. We as children spent many hours in the top fields by the crossroads bending over picking up potatoes and counting the money we would earn. The tractor would go ahead with the flailing arms of the digger opening up the ground for a hundred yards at a time and an army of hands would swoop on the exposed potatoes and put them in baskets. This would go on all day hardly without a break. Everybody slept well after potato picking and was relieved when it was all over.

At the back or side of every cottage was a vegetable patch occupying a substantial part of the garden. Where there was no man to do the work the women picked up the spade. Most households were self-sufficient in vegetables to the extent of providing greens for the winter. When spring came the chicken runs were relocated on the old cabbage patches for the chickens to feed off the remains. Nothing much was wasted. Every home was a small cottage industry surviving on preserved fruit, cured bacon, rabbits, eggs and dripping. Long hours in the fields and then in the garden added up to an arduous life for some people especially those with children. Life was faced with typical good humour so long as there was food on the table.

At times relatives from London would visit us having stepped off the train at Banbury. We would all go to meet them if allowed. On one occasion Grandad and Grandma Fisher came to stay with us and to visit Grandma's sister Aunt 'Jinny'. They had to eat pretty basic food as we did but probably better than was available in London where every available patch of land albeit park, common or railway verge was cultivated. All the cooking was done in the grate on the hob which had an oven as part of the range. Diet lacked variety and I can remember grizzling at the table over the food. Grandad was not the most patient of men having been brought up in harder times and slapped a slice of bread and marmalade into my face which mingled with the tears running down my face and produced a sorry sight as it clung in position. We never fussed at the table again and did as we were told to eat up all the food on our plate. We three children consumed a pot of jam a day on our bread to satisfy our appetites.

The bread we ate arrived once a week in Taplins van freshly cooked. It was all brown bread as there was no white flour. We longed to eat white bread again. The van stopped at the top of the lane filled with crisp loaves and cakes in paper cases. One had to be there early to be sure of a good choice.

Meat was rationed and as scarce as anywhere else despite living in the country. The butcher, Harold Hornsby, was a very small man hardly tall enough to reach over his counter top, and had his shop opposite the Pantins on Brook Road going up to the village greens. He opened his shop for only part of the week as he had little to sell. Trying to bargain with him was almost impossible. His shop was part of the slaughter house at the rear but it made no difference to his supply of meat as it was strictly regulated. The same rules did not apply to the animals going to slaughter. It was as if they knew it was their end. On one occasion a bull escaped and ran round like a demented beast. We all scattered in fright and the bull pursued us into the Pantins garden charging anything that moved including gates and fences that got in the way. It went like a bull to slaughter, unwilling, bad-tempered and intent on revenge. It seemed hours before it was caught. We were lucky to escape. So were the Pantins whose son John was in a wheelchair, disfigured and with a speech impediment which was made worse by the fright he experienced. His younger sister and brother, Olive and Leonard took care of him fortunately.

Just by the slaughter house was a laurel bank where we used to play and hide. We were quick to learn the local 'customs' and to my mind it was an ideal place to play 'dicks' with 'guess who' so I would wait for her in the bushes. As luck would have it she came down the hill one day and I succeeded in enticing her into the bushes but failed due to shyness to have anything but a chat and she was on her way again. It was not always bad luck though as cousin Brian and I somehow ended up at Ledwell Pit with 'guess who' one day. On a ledge in the pit we played mothers and fathers by taking off our clothes,'mum' with her legs out flat and with me on top carrying on like a father-to-be. Brian could not be persuaded to join in so I had to play his part. I was so sore at the end that I was lucky we were disturbed by a visitor to the pit to prevent permanent damage. We just lay there hoping not to be seen, and a little frightened in case we were caught with no clothes on.

We had plenty of examples of animals behaving in such fashion from pigs to bulls whilst farmers and grown-ups stood round and watched. It was no doubt as exciting for them as it was for us to watch. One day I was nonchalantly going to work on Mr. Tustains farm and had entered the farmyard when shouts came from all directions. I took cover in a cowshed as it was evident my life was in danger. A jersey cow was in the farmyard about to be inseminated by a jersey bull when I happened upon the scene. Jersey bulls are reputedly ferocious animals and would have made short work of me had I been in the open. I stood and watched behind the barrier occasionally taking a glance into the next stall where another bull, this time a fresian, was snorting away.

Most of the open air activities took place on the village green by the Old Road with the spreading chestnut tree as the centre piece and the Falkland Arms close at hand. There was often a Maypole Dance for us to perform accompanied by a May Queen. She was elected by popular vote of the children at school where the dance was taught on a frame around a tree in the playground. Mavis Clifton was made Queen one year and sister Maureen was Maid of Honour which caused great jealousy. The girls and the boys made daisy chains and parents made dresses for the girls either in green or different colours to match the garland of flowers worn as a headdress. Tables were also erected for cake stalls and cake competitions. The judges were not allowed to know who had made the cakes and it was always expected that a villager would win. When mother won the prize for the best cake and later adjudged by the American soldiers to have the best ankles on display at a competition held in the School Hall she became the most unpopular woman in the village at least in the eyes of the other women.

A short distance away on the side of the green were the allotments. On one festive day we stood and watched another pig being slaughtered this time by having its throat cut. When the blood had drained away it was roasted on a spit with its bristles crackling as the flames leapt up to meet it. By then we were beginning to accept it as matter of fact.

We were also invited to attended events at Little Tew. There was at sometime a play in the village hall after which tea and cakes were served. On another occasion we were expected to do the Maypole Dance at fairs held at The Grange having been well rehearsed at school for hours on end. The music would begin and we would skip along to the music weaving in and out to form a pattern at the top of the Maypole. One was not supposed to make a mistake for if anyone did one ended up in an awful mess. That is just what happened as I missed a move and put everybody else out. At the end of the dance instead of unwinding to the starting point with our single tapes straight up the pole we had to let them go to unravel themselves. We received polite applause for our efforts and I received impolite reprimands for mine. I think that was the last Maypole danced by the team. Not to be outdone sister Maureen joined in the bun fight literally. With hands behind her back the object was to eat a bun hanging from a string. Well, with a little help from her chin, it fell off so she finished eating it grovelling on the grass to everybody's amusement and won a prize for herself. All these events were for raising money for the war not to start local wars which they often did when feelings ran high. Despite the ups and downs the sun always seemed to shine to make the day a success.

 The worst days for us three children were Sundays as we had to attend the Church right at the top end of the village. It was a long way to walk all up hill, all dressed up for the service and all by ourselves as the villagers did not appear to go to Church. They just listened to the bells as they rang to mark Sunday and worked on their day of rest going possibly to Evensong. Church for the villagers meant by and large special occasions like births, Christenings, marriages, harvest festivals, Christmas carols services and burials. Every Sunday we sat there in the Church on our own, a congregation of three ready with our total offertory of 9 old pence, until months later when we were joined by the 'cripples' from the Manor House. They arrived in their flock to occupy a separate part of the church followed by the vicar who was the last to arrive. We were cold, bored, and felt hard done-by. We learnt every hymn off by heart, listened to every sermon and were brought up to behave like decent folk but to no avail. However, we always behaved in Church as one would have expected even though the vicar was a long way off. After Church we would venture forth and arrive home eventually in a dirty state to be told off for ruining our best clothes.

 A little way down the hill from the Church was the Blacksmiths which we would often visit. It was in the middle of a terrace of cottages with a big open door. The blacksmith, Mr Gibbard, was always a busy man and kept himself to himself. There were few horses in the village to be shod and he

St. Michael's Church

The Manor House from St. Michael's Church.

served the whole area. We would go in to see him blowing with his bellows to raise the flames and watch him working on a horseshoe on his anvil shaping the shoe and making it sizzle on the horses foot before plunging it into cold water. At times he would wrestle with a horses foot because the animal would not stand still. He had many a scar to show for his trouble. Living and working near to the Church could not save any man from misfortune however righteous he might have been as life seemed kinder to children who had, on balance, a better chance of escaping ill-fortune.

Semblance Of Order

Chapter 6

Amidst the chaos of war on the continent life in the village went on as normally as possible. There was the school, the Manor House, the Church and the pub to occupy villagers with different interests according to age.

The school was positioned squarely in the middle of the village on one floor standing solidly if not resplendently in its pale brown and yellow stone above the pub and the surrounding cottages. It was a proud building with an assembly hall and one classroom to take the few pupils attending. The one teacher Mrs. Lamprey had to teach a range of children from 5 to 11 as one class. Consequently, there was little advancement above the basics which was sufficient or so it was thought for the local children as they would be the next generation to supply labour to the numerous farms. No great academic achievement seemed necessary although some pupils did go on to achieve a vocation but mostly ended up at the secondary school at 'Chippy'.

We, as evacuees, had no choice. It was that or be bombed somewhere else. I can remember doing some simple mathematics and some geography. Certainly a lot of drawing was done in crayons but my greatest achievement was making raffia mats indoors and outdoors on the grass when the sun was shining. The teacher seemed to have an obsession with raffia mats of all sizes and it must have appealed to her nature to spend time going round and round in circles as befitting a full life. School plays were evidently thought to be an ideal educational tool. For one play I had to dress up wrapped completely in blue paper as Little Boy Blue whilst others were dressed as nursery rhyme characters which was a complete embarrassment. The play was performed in front of parents with paper unwrapping as I struggled on, with lines forgotten and children sobbing their way through the singing. I was glad I was not a parent.

The best time at school was play time when one could make as much noise as one liked and play with the girls. Half the time in the classroom was spent being called to order and writing love notes to friends saying you loved them and asking did they love you. That was not what we were used to. We all knew George loved sister Maureen or so he said and I loved Mavis but was told by her in a note she did not love me but loved cousin Brian. The notes read "Do you love me?" and if you did you signed on the dotted line. So it went on. Life was full of trial and error. That was how relationships in the village were cemented by likes and dislikes and whether you were 'clean' or not. For us Londoners it was a rude awakening.

The Misses Bolton owned the Manor House at Tew Park overlooking the village. The Government requisitioned the estate to take handicapped evacuees from Croydon which had been devastated in bombing raids. The children and staff including teachers were transferred from temporary accommodation in Littlehampton. The Bolton sisters had to move back to live in Ringmer leaving the gardeners who belonged to the estate and Miss Monk in charge of operations who lived near the Blacksmiths. Mrs. Coleman was the chief cook and Margaret Breadfast did the mending for the children helped by a small army of people doing housekeeping. Aunty Margaret was on her way to Tew when war broke out on 3rd September, 1939 and worked there later volunteering her services at the Manor House rather than do factory work.

Apart from farming, work in the village came to revolve around the Manor House with so many villagers helping out after the children arrived. Those that were able were to be seen going out in crocodile walks hobbling behind each other in their calipers and in an array of leather supports to keep them mobile. It was a sorry sight seeing the walking wounded and poking fun at them was a cruel game. They deserved better as they were alone in the world and in the church and were never allowed to join in the village life because of the strict rules that governed their social behavior outside the Manor. Some effort was made to make them feel welcome as we, for example, at Brookside entertained Maureen Horne and Freda Bryant, both orphans, to tea one day. Freda wore calipers which she was persuaded to take off and hand round for inspection.

To entertain the residents and to aid the Red Cross, garden parties, dances and whist drives were held at the Manor House and similar social functions were organised at the Village Hall before it was burnt down. Tew Park, as it was also called, was an ideal setting for children's games behind the house on the lawns which were always kept in perfect condition. At a fancy dress party for all children sister Maureen went as a traffic light, Mavis was dressed as a golly wog and George ran off so to speak with the first prize dressed as Ghandi in sandals that were far too big for him.

Tew Park was laid out in lawns bedecked with mature ornamental trees. It was a place of peace and recreation surrounded by a stone wall broken only by the iron cattlegate to the village, the double-sized gate for the drive and the wooden door to the Church yard. On the path to the Church one passed the tennis court. The court was the warren for a family of rabbits who came out to play whenever Aunty Margaret and mother decided to have a game. It was not the sort of game they had in mind.

The Church served the villagers only for Christenings, weddings, funerals and harvest festivals. I can only remember harvest festivals ever

Tew Park Staff

L to R. 1st row.

- Leslie Arnold
- Ivor Brooks
- Robin Leach
- Valerie Allen
- Valerie Ayler
- Joyce Burner
- Shirley Robinson
- John Johnson
- Dennis Lane
- Robin Prentice
- John Holliday

L to R. 2nd row.

- Mrs Slatter
- Miss Pesend
- Miss Ryell
- Sister
- Mrs Haley
- Mrs Brooks
- Miss Suckling
- Miss Lambert
- Miss Hainsworth
- Miss Robinson
- Miss Holt

L to R. 3rd row.

- Gordon Burns
- Sara Adams
- June Edwards
- Carol Hern
- Vivien Stringer
- Roy Harding
- Jim Turner
- John Harvey
- John Lock
- Leonard Bailey
- Harold Edwards
- Michael
- Mrs Harris

L to R. Back Row.

- Tom Wright
- Harry Louder
- Joan Shields
- Derek Peek
- Andrew Crawford
- Donald Pett
- Lilian Mitchell
- Pat Gatland
- Edward Dix
- Eileen Boxer
- Wendy Stamms

taking place and the funeral for Michael Lowe. There were no weddings as I recollect.

The bus service from Worths at Enstone provided a lifeline to the outside world. The Saturday morning bus to 'Chippy' was always full. Occasionally the children went by themselves in which case there was fun and games. Shortly after our arrival we had our first introduction to condoms which were provided by George Clifton who had come across them at home. We, in our innocence, thought they were balloons but when we were told their real purpose the pleasure they gave us for being naughty was even greater as they floated around the bus and as we waved them out the window. When, on occasions, the parents joined the children we went our own ways in the town. There was plenty to do and buy from soft drinks to the choice of two cinemas and even a market in the town centre on both sides of the street. The top cinema was the better of the two showing such delights as 'Gone With The Wind' which we saw at a very young age. The bottom cinema boasted more basic pleasures guaranteed to frighten the life out of a child with suspense and horror such as it was. All was forgotten on the way home in the bus when malt loaves or the like were torn to pieces to satisfy ravenous appetites.

Getting to the village during the war required a masterpiece of planning to make the connections and demands on the feet were legion. If one had a car like Aunty Margaret life was easier but with a ration of two gallons a week not a great advantage. That all came to an end when the petrol allowance was revoked in 1942. The car was then just laid up in a garage adjoining the Falkland Arms. Father had to travel from Bath which he did by catching the Black and White coach to the Banbury Road getting off by the Masons Arms and walking the two miles to the village. We would walk there to meet him, Maureen going along expecting to receive a Mars bar at the end of her walk. On another day, Christmas Day, father met two lorry drivers at the Masons Arms and brought them home for Christmas Dinner to save himself walking. They drove their enormous lorry down the lane and stayed most of the day sharing what little food mother had prepared for us, taking the best seats and bouncing us on their laps with great amusement.

Father was also to have his bad days. His luck ran out when Gerald Crook was born at 2 o'clock in the morning. With only a bicycle available he cycled the three miles to Enstone to fetch the District Nurse who jumped in her car to drive to the village leaving father to cycle all the way back again much to his annoyance.

The Yanks Are Coming

Chapter 7

The strategic plans for the North Africa landings on 8th November, 1942 for operation 'Torch' were a secret. All we knew was that the Yanks were coming. Their arrival was marked by the the rumble of isolated tanks coming along the road from the descent of Banbury Hill. We went to meet them on the road between Butchers Hill and Banbury Hill which by-passed the village. We had gone there to scrounge chewing gum and army ration chocolate as that was what our cousins said they had to offer. We called out as they passed "Have you got any gum chum" and we were now and then suitably rewarded by having some thrown to us. On the whole though the occupants of the tanks just stood up waving as the noise deafened our calls.

The Sherman tanks were transported from America to England by boat and landed at Liverpool or Southampton. They were then dispersed throughout the south of England. It was all very secretive in the latter part of 1941. Soon however the whole countryside seemed to be swarming with them as they set about spreading themselves out across the fields that were accessible to the lanes. A large contingent settled on Cow Hill taking some sort of cover under the trees and churning up the fields especially around the gates to the fields. When it rained the ground became very boggy and tracks and mud were left on every road. The lorries for the invasion were all hidden away with more care in woods at Shipton-under-Wychwood. The main roads to the towns were lined with piles of shells for mile after mile ready for the action to come.

Being children we just walked around unhindered to satisfy our curiosity and to talk to the troops. They seemed to be stationed there for some time, it seemed like years but was only for about nine months. In that time they kept away from the village as it was out-of-bounds but nevertheless they managed to spread their bonhomie to the female population. Transport, in the form of American lorries, was laid on for the ladies to attend dances once a month at Hook Norton or Stow-on-the-Wold. There seemed no shortage of chocolates and cigarettes, mostly Camels, 200 at a time for those that wanted such luxuries. The dance bands suffered no shortage of food. How could the ladies resist such and other temptations?

About that time Mrs Marquetus moved from the village green by the well to a cottage in the lane between Cow Hill and the bottom of Banbury

Hill and her reputation moved with it. By then she had become the mother of three children all of whom lived in fairly squalid conditions as we saw it. She was not the only one to be the subject of gossip as any woman without a husband present and certainly any widow naturally socialised more freely. By all accounts the womenfolk were having a good time for the first time in many years.

A Kind Of Graduation

Chapter 8

The village school had no past record of academic achievement by its pupils. In fact the curriculum and the quality of its teacher Mrs. Lamprey were factors against any success except having happy days at school. Despite the odds being against her Mrs. Lamprey was going to have her moment of glory. The time came when the older boys were to take their 11 Plus Examination to enter or not the Grammar School at Chipping Norton. Brother Raymond was one of her favourite pupils as it happened. When sitting his paper Mrs Lamprey read his answers to check how well he had done. Not perfectly well apparently. So, she said, "Raymond, that that and that and that answer was not correct." and told him what they should be which he duly corrected. What a surprise. When the results were announced he had scored the highest marks of 100. Somewhere along the way 'Rake' had also acquired the title of 'Professor' which he then deserved. With such high qualifications Raymond entered the Grammar School swearing to keep the secret. Not long after Miss Wyatt took over the school from Mrs Lamprey. It was in later years we read in the newspapers that Mrs. Lamprey had been allegedly caught on an embezzlement charge and put in prison. What a fine example to set innocent minds!

As Raymond had succeeded I, being his brother, had an advantage and was given the privilege of entering the same school after sitting an entrance examination whatever the result turned out to be. I do not remember doing very well but Mr. Coomber, 'Booty' as we called him, let me enter the school. He was to regret that decision in the short time we were there.

Now Raymond and I were, so to speak, underprivileged children, without the resources available to a smaller family and without an attentive and attendant father. It struck Raymond that we could acquire the status of owning a marbled propelling pen by taking one out of a desk in another classroom when everybody was out of the way at break time. We told our mother that we had found them at Ledwell Pit which she believed as we were always bringing useful things home from there. Eventually we were caught as pupils identified their pens as well as other things in Raymond's possession. The discovery of our theft brought about our suspension from school. I was suspended from school for one week and Raymond for two. The news soon reached the ears of people in the village and we were all sent to 'Coventry'. When words were exchanged there was no doubt about the shame and disgrace we had brought upon ourselves and the village. If the stocks on The Green had been in better condition and it had been a different era we would have been put in them for sure.

Not all the news of the family's escapades reached the village. After school at 'Chippy' we would often go into the town centre to do a little 'shopping'. Just past the Town Hall was Woodhouse's shop that sold watches and clocks. All the valuables were kept in show cases and glass-topped counters. By distracting the shopkeeper it was possible to reach round and take ones pick. I can recall being envious of owning a watch and managed on the day to take two without being noticed and left the shop with them. Later our mother discovered our possessions and extracted a confession from us. She was distraught with grief naturally. Some time later she devised a plan to return the watches to their rightful owner by waiting in trepidation outside the shop until the coast was clear and then slipping inside quietly to place them on the counter and make a hasty retreat. No message or apology was left. All that was left was a bad memory and two nearly new watches.

We had always walked the five miles to Chipping Norton to attend County school come rain, snow or sunshine as the daily school bus from Enstone only picked up pupils from the surrounding villages attending the secondary school at 'Chippy' as they finished at 4 pm and we at 4.30 pm. In the winter months it was miserable. Eventually the Government decided to be very generous to Raymond and me and Alan Morley so we thought. So, to help us on our way we were given bicycles to go to 'Chippy' daily to attend school. I remember his bicycle was a Federal and mine a Daws. Raymond's was a lump of heavy iron with poor brakes which he was to discover to his cost. One day coming down Butchers Hill as fast as he could go as usual he tried to negotiate the corner at the bottom, past the triangle where two large beech trees grew. He missed the first tree but not the second and having skidded on the gravel went head first into the tree. He was never quite the same person after that. Apart from writing off the bike and making a mess of his knees, legs and elbows on the gravel he did eventually get a replacement bicycle. By then he had really earned the title of 'Rake'.

In 1944 Uncle Bill had been sent home from the war after the campaigns in North Africa and in Italy suffering from duodenal ulcers. He spent three months recuperating in the Radcliffe Hospital in Oxford some time before VE-Day on 8th May, 1945. In about August that year Bill started working on his old Morris 8 in the garages across the lane from the Falkland Arms and I helped him to strip down the car to make it roadworthy again. As a reward for my efforts he gave me a jackknife which was a treasured possession and better than any toy.

The time was nearing to say goodbye to life in the country which still offered no tap water or electricity until its late and first arrival at the council estate at the top of Butchers Hill. Such services had passed by the village. Even the radios had to have their accumulator batteries replaced or recharged to keep in touch with the world as we sat there listening to the radio playing such tunes as 'You Are My Sunshine' with all four of us occupied with our knitting. There were no street lights and the merest hint of light through the window in the blackout invited at least one knock on the door from an out-of-town policeman.

One sad morning in the late Autumn of 1945 some weeks after our cousins had left for London, we had loaded up our removal van including 'Snarler' the cat. The tailgate swung up and we slowly made our departure past the Cliftons with only Mavis managing to wave and went up the hill from Brookside. Nobody intentionally turned out to wave goodbye except 'Crackers' Crook who ran after us until he reached the butchers shop and ran no more. It was the end of 5 years of occupation and the end of an era. We had left our mark during our relatively brief invasion of the village which was to retreat once again into living in the past.

Profile of Great Tew

A Brief History.

Great Tew sits on the edge of the Cotswolds in a geological region known as the Swerford Beds. The south side of the village is built on limestone and the northern side between the ironstone valleys. The origins of the village pre-date the Domesday Book of 1086 when, due to its early ecclesiastical importance, it was known as Cyrictiwa (Church Tew). At the time of the Domesday Book, Great Tew had become Tewam and had belonged to the Bishop of Bayeux who until 1082 had been the greatest feudal landowner in the county. He had acquired the estate from the Abbey of St. Albans to whom it was bequeathed by the Archbishop of Canterbury in 1003 or 1004. The present Church of St Michael stands partly on the foundations of the 12th century Norman Church as a reminder of its earlier religious origin.

The parish originally included Little Tew and Duns Tew but by the time the Bishop died in 1097 the whole estate had disintegrated and separate baronies had been created. During the next century the Great Tew estate was to be retrieved by the Crown several times. By 1238 three Lords namely, des Preaux, de Vere and de Somery owned the three manors in Great Tew. Open fields were in two-course cultivation divided unequally into West and North fields and South and East fields. In 1279 there were 53 recorded households half of whom fell victim to the plague with further devastation caused later by the the Black Death both of which occurred in the 14th century.The separate manors continued intact until the des Preaux manor passed through marriage to Henry Rainsford in 1450 whose family had by 1536 acquired all three manors to make a single estate. During the 16th century, the village fell into disrepair as a direct result of eliminating freeholds and creating leases for years or for life under the Rainsford family whose descendants survived until 1611. In 1550 to 1580 Tew Park was established followed by the building of the 'old' E-shaped Manor House.

In 1611 Sir Lawrence Tanfield purchased the estate and was in trouble with farmers and Parliament for his inclosure activities. His death in 1626 coincided with doubling of the death rate due again to the plague. He was succeeded by his grandson Lucius Cary, later to become Lord Falkland who met his death in 1643 at the battle of Newbury. As the century drew to a close the population numbers had probably recovered to 13th century levels and the village had been rebuilt by individual smallholders and tenants most of whom were small farmers. The building work included Court Farm, Leys Farm, the Falkland Arms (which was probably then the Horse and Groom), many of the cottages facing The Green and the Old Road and the row of cottages by the vicarage.

In 1698 the estate was purchased by Francis Keck and was passed to his nephew, John Tracy, in 1728, who had to adopt the name 'Keck' to succeed to the title. He was probably the person responsible for planting the T-shaped avenue of trees $1^1/_2$ miles long connecting the Manor in a direct line towards Banbury. By 1761 the arable land was under 8 year rotation but the Inclosure Act of 1766 deprived smallholders of their livelihood when short leases were cancelled in order to enhance the value of Keck's estate. In the 1770's several local roads were turnpiked. The end of the male line in the Keck family forced sale of the estate.

The estate came into the hands of George Stratton in 1778 who by 1793 had bought the remainder. He and his descendants were to influence the development and later isolation of the village. A road was built connecting the Crossroads to the Banbury Road and the 'old' Manor House was demolished. Stratton employed an agriculturalist, named Loudon, whose Scottish farming experiments failed but who succeeded in transforming the northern landscape. Hedgerows were grubbed up leaving the trees on the hills, trees were planted, ponds and a mill were built, much of the tree-lined avenue was destroyed and as a result thirteen farms were vacant in 1814. In the same year the new Manor House was built which compelled the villagers to adopt an indirect route to the Church.

As the farming experiment was such a disaster and as the value of the land had inflated so much, Stratton decided to sell to M.R.Boulton in 1816. Under Boulton and his heirs the village witnessed a most radical change which took place in two rebuilding phases. The first, between 1816 and 1844, saw the infilling of gaps to create rows of cottages, tree planting throughout the village and a new link road was made to the Square. During the second phase in the 1850's the New Road was laid to connect the top of the village to The Green and the Old Road was cut off below the Manor House. Many of the farms were amalgamated leaving 6 principal ones. The number of houses rose to 102 by 1891 but the population fell to 334 by 1901.

When M.R.Boulton died in 1914 life interests were acquired by his two resident sisters, Clara and Margaret, and the estate was administered by the

Public Trustee for the next 50 years.

At the outbreak of war in 1939 there were three shops in the village. The bomber base was established at Enstone, evacuees were housed in the village, orphans from Croydon were cared for at the Manor House and for most of the year in 1943 the American Forces were stationed on Cow Hill. Electricity was also brought to part of the village.

Under the Public Trustee little was done to prevent a decline in the estate as cottages and buildings fell into decay and were abandoned. By 1951 the population had declined to 204. Later, in 1962 Major Eustace Robb inherited the estate and there was then a recovery in farming, a sewage plant was built and piped water was connected. The policy was to restore the village for the rural community but the plan failed as more and more cottages became derelict in the 1970's. The population numbered 211 in 1971. The controversy continued at a local and national level until 1978 when the village was declared a Conservation Area. However, that was not a remedy for restoration of the village. In the 1980's the dereliction continued until people from outside the village were allowed to buy properties rightly or wrongly and restore them to their present day appearance.

May 1976

⇑   *May 1991*   ⇓

Map created from the place names in the Domesday Survey.

Reproduced from the *Victoria County History: Oxfordshire*. Volume 1 by permission of the General Editor

Great Tew

A 1000 years of History.

It lies 16 miles from Oxford 8 miles from Banbury and 5 miles from Chipping Norton

It is some 10 miles in circumference and includes the parish of Little Tew.

Most of the material in this section is extracted from the <u>Victoria County History: Oxfordshire,</u> *Volume I, pages 363-428, and Volume XI, pages 223-247.*

- 990 Aelfric, Abbot of St Albans, was the earliest known holder as a single manor which may have included Little Tew and Duns Tew.
- 995-1005 Aelfric was to become the Archbishop of Canterbury.
- 1003-1004 Aelfric, in his will, bequeathed Great Tew to the Abbey of St.Albans.
- 1000-1035 The village was known as Church Tew (Cyrictiwa)which reflected its importance as an early ecclesiastical centre. The parish included Little Tew which continued until 1857.
- 1042-1066 At the time of Edward the Confessor Great Tew was still known as 'Cyrictiwa'.
- post 1066 The land was seized from Alnod of Kent and given to Odo, Bishop of Bayeux, by personal grant from William 1.
- pre 1082 Traditionally it is believed that Paul, Abbot of St.Albans, secured the return of Great Tew from Odo but was compelled by William 11 (probably William 1 who reigned 1066-1087) to grant it to Hugh de Envermeu. Finally the claim was abandoned by Abbot Richard and the parish was returned to Odo.
- 1082-1097 Odo had been under arrest since 1082 who was by then the greatest landlord in Oxfordshire.
- 1086 The Domesday Survey (Book) was commissioned to record land ownership for tax collection and mentions Great Tew (Tewam), Little Tew (Teowe) and Dunstew (also Teowe).
- 1086 Great Tew was assessed as 16 hides in 1086 and 1130 but was probably 25 hides, to correspond with land for 26 plough teams, as later evidence supports the oversight of 9 hides by the Domesday commissioners. (The ancient family lands were known in English as 'hides' which was the basis of early taxation-Oxfordshire contained exactly 2400 hides).
- 1086 There were 53 recorded tenants in the village.
- 1086 The pasture recorded in the Book was probably at Cow Hill.
- 1086 There were 288 acres of meadow recorded of which some 215 acres were in Great Tew.
- 1097 On Odo's death in 1097, if not before, his whole estate was disintegrated and

	separate baronies were created. Great Tew came into the hands of Hugh de Envermeu.
1118	Upon the death of Hugh de Envermeu between 1111 and 1118 it reverted to King Henry 1 where it remained until 1130.
1130	The Crown then lost possession for a time.
1165	Great Tew was then recovered by Henry 11 but a portion of the manor seems to have been kept by Randulph, Earl of Chester.
1189	After Richard 1 succeeded to the throne he gave Great Tew to Ernulf de Mandeville who was on crusade with him.
1194	It then reverted to the Crown again.
1196	The records show that it was then held by William de Hundescote possibly a Flemish knight in royal service.
1189-1199	The records then conflict as Randolph, Earl of Chester must have owned the larger portion of Great Tew and part of the manor, possibly from King Richard 1 who was on the throne at the time or from William de Hundescote.
1204	Part of the manor was held by Hugh de Colonces which upon forfeiture reverted to Randulph, Earl of Chester.
1206	The other and larger portion of Great Tew was granted by the Earl to John des Preaux probably one of his knights in royal service in Normandy thus creating the first manor.
1206	An advowson was given with the manor to John des Preaux and later in 1302 it was granted to Godstow Abbey which presented the first vicar in 1309. The advowson was retained until the Dissolution when it was granted by the Crown in 1541 to William Rainsford.
1226-1230	The Earl gave land at Tew to Baldwin de Vere thus creating the second manor.
1226	There were 2 watermills for corn. The one in the Vere manor was in the south and the other in the Preaux manor was in the north along Mill Lane.
1232	What remained of the Earls lands at his death was allotted to one of his coheirs Hugh D'Aubigny, Earl of Arundel.
1238	The Earl then gave the land to his sister upon marriage to Roger de Somery thus creating the third manor. The three Lords owning the manors were Vere, Somery and Preaux plus a freeholding of William of Chalgrove.
1238-1302	Many of the Church rectors were members of the des Preaux family.
13th Century.	Management of the land was by way of open fields in two-course cultivation located in four fields of unequal size. The West and North fields seem to have been cultivated together and the South with East. South field was apparently the largest. North and East fields probably touched in the area north of the park where the land slopes down to the streams. Nearly all the freeholds were held by the Preaux manor but little is known of their creation.
1249	There were only 6 free tenants with 11 yardlands (a yardland being 1232 x 1241 but varying from 3 to 9¼ acres according to field), a mill and 10 cottages or cotlands on the three manors.
1268 & 1288	The Lords of Little Tew protested against the des Preaux practice of

making a hitch crop on the boundaries of the village as it interfered with their right to pasture on the fallow of Great Tew.

1279 John des Preaux had power to hang a thief on his gallows. Courts leet and baron were held in the village until the early 19th century.

1279 There were at least 53 recorded households and 85 recorded yardlands to which should be added 4 yardlands of glebe, 6 ploughlands of demesne and some cottage holdings making a possible total of over 2300 acres under plough probably near the maximum possible. By the end of the century the fields were probably fully developed.

14th Century. There was heavy depopulation although its impact is not recorded.

1303 The de Vere estate in Tew had passed from Baldwin de Vere to his brother John de Vere in 1279 and then to his son Robert who in 1303 mortgaged it, finally being held by Roger Chaunteclere who sold it in 1338 by an exchange to Thomas Purcell. It then continued in the Purcel family until 1491-2 when it was sold to Richard Hall thereafter passing to his son, a lunatic, before being acquired by William Rainsford in 1536.

1309 A vicarage was created by Godstow Abbey and the first vicar was ordained.

1333 There appeared to be comparatively little Domesday meadow left due to encroachment.

1333 On the death of Ralph des Preaux the Crown claimed Tew as a royal demesne reviving a claim of 1249.

1341-1342 William, son and heir of Ralph des Preaux, vindicated his title to Tew but his guardian had in 1340 granted a life interest to Amice Chelmscote. The estate then passed through marriage to Henry Rainsford in 1450. Thus began the Rainsford Dynasty.

14th Century. There was considerable population loss presumably through plague (transmitted by fleas and rats) and which killed off perhaps half the population of Europe. In the period between 1348 and 1350 the Black Death further contracted the population of Great Tew which left part of the land uncultivated encouraging some early inclosure.

1377 Those assessed for poll tax had been reduced to 165 adults.

1398 The des Preaux manor had passed to Alice, wife of John Wilcotes.

1413 On Alice's death John Wilcotes married Elizabeth who after his death in 1422 retained a life interest until 1439 or later. Upon expiry of the life interest, John's will passed the manor to their daughter who had married Henry Rainsford before 1450.

by 1422 The process of creating freeholds had been reversed as there were only 6 freeholds, 10 yardlands and a mill with at most 3 free tenants of peasant stock.

1439-50 The manor passed to Henry Rainsford.

1488 William, son of Henry Rainford, died in possession of the manor.

1488-1611 The estate then descended from father to son for several generations of the Rainsford family.

1500-1650 There were numerous crafts carried on by carpenters, masons, blacksmiths of the Barnes family, tailors, a chapman and a mercer.

1500-1699 Like most other villages in the region Great Tew following a period of

disrepair and was rebuilt by individual householders having been in single ownership by mid 16th century. Tenants held leases for lives. The population had probably recovered to 13th century levels.

1524 Richard Busby paid two thirds of the taxes on the parish which overshadowed those paid by the Rainsfords, father and son.

1536 William, grandson of William Rainsford, had inherited the Rainsford estate and purchased during his father John's lifetime the de Vere estate from the Hall family of Swerford having previously been owned by the Purcel family.

1541 William Rainsford purchased from the Crown part of the des Preaux estate which was a large freehold created before 1249 consisting of 8 yardlands given by Rainsford on the marriage of his daughter.

1550-1580 Tew Park was created absorbing some of the cottages behind its walls which isolated the Church and Manor House from the village. The medieval street (Old Road) linking the village to the Church was presumably deflected round the site. By 1599 the park had been divided into three sections: Inner, Middle and Outer Parks. In the late 18th century it was to become a deer park.

1575-1610 The Old E-shaped Manor House was built with the main front to the south with the walled garden on the west and the Church on the east. The west wing was extended southwards to eight bays perhaps later in the 17th century.

1598 Portions of the park were sometimes let and occasionally ploughed.

by 1600 The late medieval trend towards the elimination of freeholds had continued under the Rainsfords and by the 17th century Great Tew was almost all in single ownership. The Lane and Brook Road leading from The Green had been established.

1611 Edward Rainsford sold Great Tew to Sir Laurence Tanfield, Chief Baron of the Exchequer.

1615 The wills of farmers show they were content to divide their long leases for years or lives to their sons and some 100 yardlands were willed between 1557 and 1736.

1622 The land was valued for inclosure. The northern part, North field, Horse hill, Cotman mead and Cow hill were to be valued as grass or 'sward ground' and the southern as arable. On inclosure $23^{1}/_{2}$ acres were allotted for each yardland or $21^{1}/_{2}$ if common pasture was taken into account.

1622 Sir Laurence began by grazing large flocks of sheep on Cow hill instead of using his own scattered strips. Tenants objected after arbitrators awarded in favour of Sir Laurence and fences were broken but the new inclosure stayed forming a continuous swathe round the north and east sides of the parish. Open fields however comprised 79 yardlands until parliamentary inclosure in 1767 which disposed of 1779 acres.

1624 & 1625 There were 24 and 18 burials respectively compared with the norm of 10 to 12. Many of the 1625 deaths were due to the plague, the first being buried in the field.

1624 The behaviour of Sir Laurence Tanfield (grandparent of Lord Falkland) came briefly to the attention of Parliament over his inclosure activities and

his case was weakened by complaints elsewhere.
1626 Sir Laurence Tanfield died.
1629 Tanfield's wife died and Great Tew passed by settlement to the grandchild Henry Cary later to become Viscount Falkland.
1630's Falkland gathered around him a witty and cultured circle and Lettice his wife probably had a more direct impact on the life of the village through her care for poor and sick villagers. She provided a school and contrived a policy of employment on her estate. Falkland's tenants held leases for lives and it was unlikely that any charitable rebuilding occurred under Falkland.
1643 Lord Falkland was killed at the battle of Newbury but was not buried at the Church.
1647 Lettice held the manor until her death.
1647-1694 She was followed by the three sons, Lucius (died 1649),Henry (died 1663) and by Henry's son Anthony(died 1694) who had no surviving children.
1660's The Quakers were prominent at this time and 2 were arrested at meetings in Bloxham. Between 1689 and 1729 some 6 Quakers were fined repeatedly for refusing tithes.
1662 Assessments of hearth tax confirm the impression of a community of small farmers under a single powerful landlord, Lord Falkland.
1662-1673 There were a number of craftsmen including bakers, shoemakers, a weaver, a fuller and a cottage belonging to Alice Hiorn where tape, thread, treacle and nails were sold.
1666 The Swan Inn is mentioned.
1670 Farmers were tending to leave the main holding, 3 yardlands, to the eldest son, a close to a second, small legacies to others and blacksmith's tools to the youngest.
1675-1696 The row of houses facing the walled garden by the present vicarage was built.
1680 Cottage No 51 in the Square was erected by John Hiorn for John Stowe. The plan and detail such as coursed rubble walls, stone mullions, plain dripmoulds and ovolo-moulded wood mullions are a common feature of 17th century or earlier building. The Falkland Arms, Court Farm, Leys Farm, No 62 at Keale's Corner and many cottages on The Green and the Old Road are examples.
1692 It seems likely that arable land was divided into quarters with rotation of 3 crops and one as fallow.
1693 Henry Cockson, the vicar, was excommunicated for marrying without banns or licence.
1698 The estate was purchased by Francis Keck from money left by his father when Sir Anthony Keck died in 1695. He acquired a reputation for good works.
1700-1799 In addition to Cow Hill which was permanent pasture, a third of the slopes of Chescombe Hill and Horse Hill (then in three divisions) was thrown open to grazing by the common herd. The radial road pattern of the village was altered to an unusual extent.

GREAT TEW 1774

Reproduced from the *Victoria County History: Oxfordshire*, Volume XI by permission of the General Editor

1700-1815 There were two Inns in Great Tew; the Pole Axe and the Horse and Groom which was held by the Worley family and which probably became the Falkland Arms.

1728 Francis Keck was said to be the "richest man and had the best estate...in Oxfordshire" and on his death as both his children were childless Tew passed to his nephew John Tracy in tail male provided he took the name Keck.

1738 The vicar reported that there were 95 houses in Great Tew.

1738 There were 4 Quaker families living in the village who probably attended the meeting at South Newington.

by 1750 The tree-lined avenue probably planted by Francis Keck, ran for over a mile in a straight line to the northern boundary at South Newington from another avenue half a mile long, connecting it to the Manor House. A 'street' in the southern half of the parish was mentioned in the 13th century and from some of the names along its path it is evident that the avenue road was once used as a direct route to Banbury.

by 1750 The remaining small freeholds had been absorbed into the estate.

1759 The vicar reported there were 92 houses in the village.

1760's There are signs that the poor were sometimes set to work on road mending.

1761 The arable land was divided into 9 sections under an 8 year rotation of turnips, barley with grass seed, hay, sheepwalk, oats, fallow, wheat and peas; the sections being 100 to 150 acres. By then the medieval system of open-field husbandry had changed beyond recognition.

1762 The small tenements held under Francis Keck of 1/4 to 3/4 yardlands amounted to 40% of the holdings. Larger units made up another 30%. As the old inclosed land was valued at three times as highly as the open-field land there was a strong incentive to Keck to proceed with inclosure and not to renew leases.

1762 John Busby one of the larger farmers on the newly inclosed land tenanted Leys Farm which remained in the family for many years but continuity in other cases seems to have been broken.

1766 The Inclosure Act cancelled all leases for rack rent under 21 years. One result of inclosure was to remove almost entirely the smallholdings that had sustained cottagers and craftsmen. A yardland then became 20 1/2 acres gross without pasture but including fieldways and common meadow which, being in stature acres, was probably larger than the field acres of medieval yardlands.

1767 Anthony the son of John Keck (Tracy) was killed at Epsom races and was succeeded by his brothers Thomas and John. In the same year the 25 acres, being one third of the Domesday meadow holding in Little Tew, held by the two Lords Vere and Somery, were disposed of in the inclosure award of Great Tew. The other two thirds previously held by des Preaux had been given away in the early 13th century.

by 1767 The Grove, south of the churchyard avenue, was well established and it was there that the 'Tew Tree' stood; a giant silver fir providing a landmark for much of the 19th century.

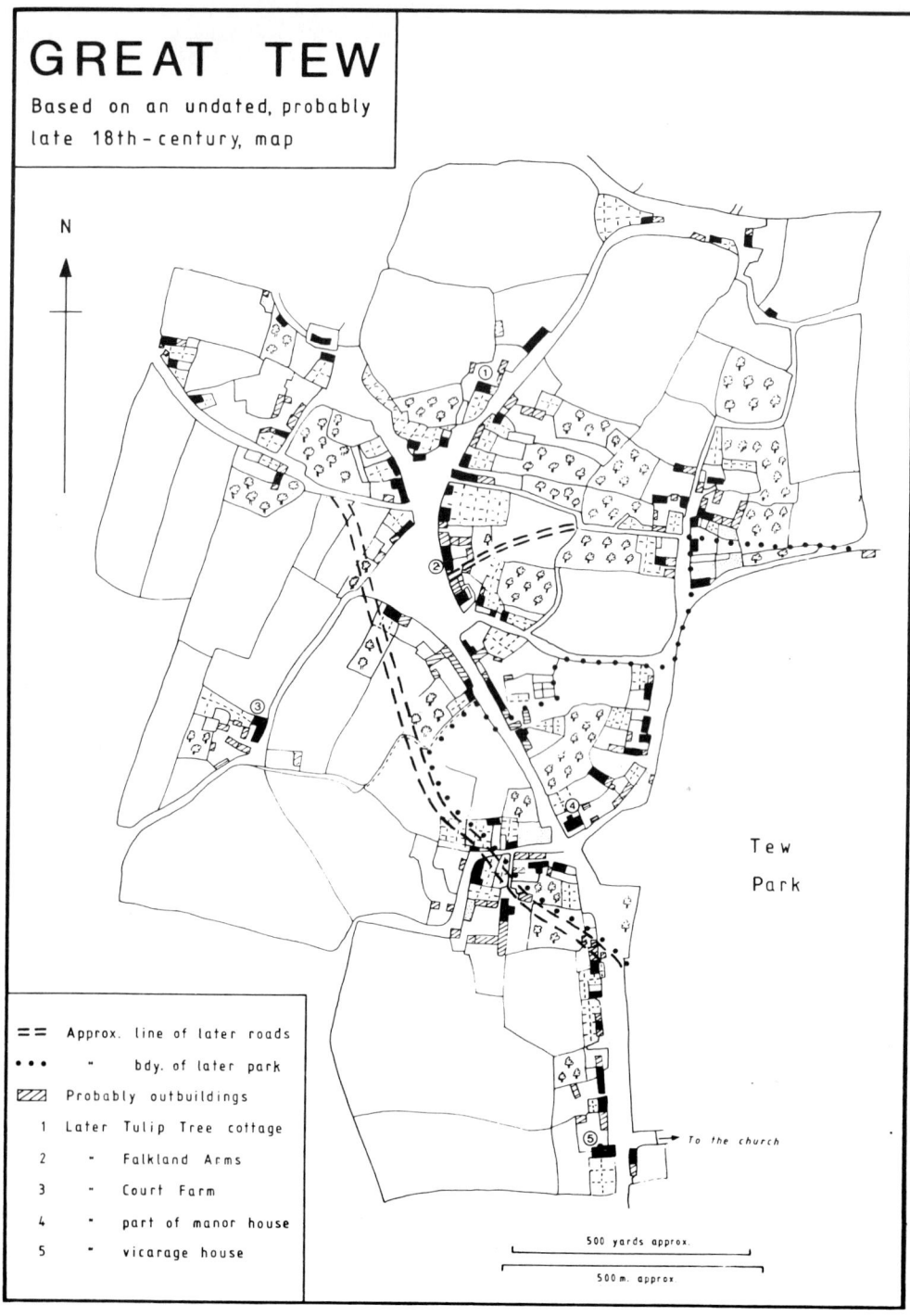

Reproduced from the *Victoria County History: Oxfordshire*, Volume XI by permission of the General Editor

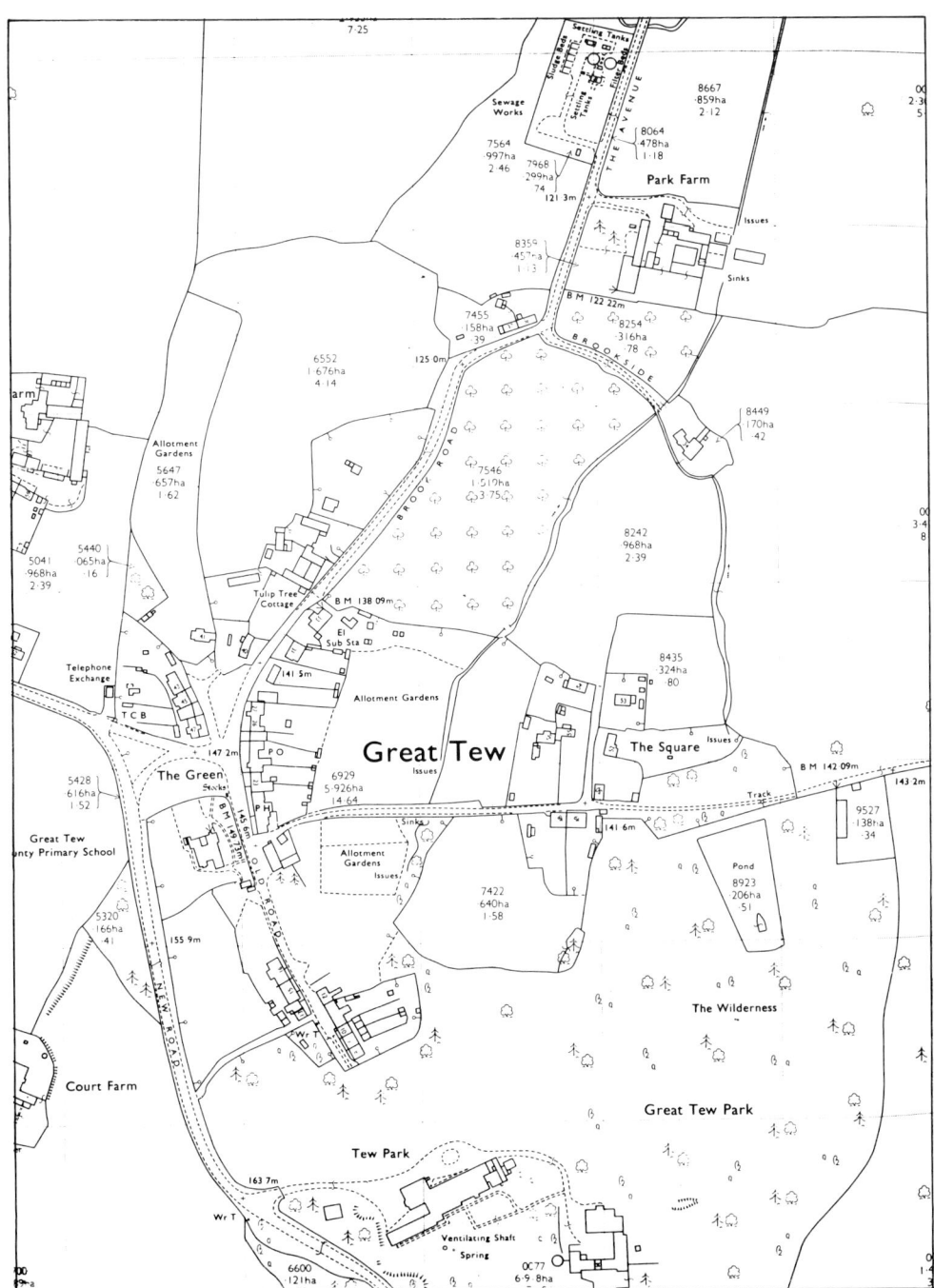

Reproduced from the Ordnance Survey (1:5000) map with permission of the Controller of HMSO. © Crown copyright

1768 The vicar reported there were 80 houses in the village.
1770 The road from Deddington to Chipping Norton was turnpiked.
1774 The lane running north past Park Farm was known as Clinkers but an earlier name was Rudaway or Rodaway, presumably 'rother way'.
1778 The Keck family had been successful inclosing land and only 3 life leases remained. The old inclosed land was divided into 4 farms, the 2 in the north both being held by the Ryman family. Most of the newly inclosed farms were still run from the village. The vicar reported there were 73 houses in the village including Tulip Tree cottage on Brook Road but few of the 18th century cottages survive.
1778 The male line failed in the Keck family in 1774 and the estate reverted to the descendants of Francis Keck's various sisters. Under a Chancery decree confirmed by a private Act in 1778 the estate was sold to avoid a complex partition between six claimants.
1780 One of the coheirs had agreed to buy the whole estate but the manor and much of the land, 2000 acres, had been acquired by George Stratton who in 1793 bought the remainder.
1781 The present vicarage house was in use but in serious disrepair by 1815. Major alterations were carried out in 1829.
1783 The village had a workhouse. Its Master William Evans died in 1793
1800 The records show that in the previous century Norton Way ran eastwards past Crimea Yard and that another road connected The Green with the Crossroads passing by Court Farm. In 1800 it was turnpiked and soon afterwards a new straight section was built from the Crossroads to join the road running north-west from the village (at the end of The Lane) to the Banbury turnpike, near the junction with Mill Lane, thus creating an early bypass.
1800 When George Stratton died the estate, free of encumbrances with its buildings in repair, was taken over by his son, G.F.Stratton, an improving landlord who surrounded it by a ring fence. Its 16 farms including those in adjoining parishes, were let on 12 year leases to allow a 6 year rotation in which fodder crops played an important part. Of the 3700 acres of farmland, 1500 acres were permanent pasture.
1800-1803 The Manor House was destroyed after neglect over succession.
1800-1814 G.F.Stratton had bought out most of the existing tenants with the intention of forming the estate into two large holdings but his Scottish agricultural experiment was to fail him.
1801-1831 Census records show that between 13 and 21 families were engaged in crafts and trades compared with 70 or more supported by agriculture.
1803-1817 There were 30 to 50 adults receiving permanent out-relief.
by 1810 Both the ancient mills were probably victims of new 'farm' mills.
1810-1811 A rented workhouse was again in use and was used as pauper housing in 1815.
1812-1813 Poor relief rose to a peak but continued at about £1 per head until 1931-1932. Many of the farms were vacant at the time.
1814 The occupation of James Gibson was Bailiff and Kitchire Maker.

1814 J. C. Loudon, the agriculturalist and gardener, had persuaded Stratton to buy out all leases or not renew them in order to adopt the Scottish system of convertible husbandry and to double the estate value. In the process the northern stretch of the tree-lined avenue was destroyed. Two large holdings were created and higher rents to tenants were raised. Quarrels ensued between Loudon and Stenhouse Wood and the over-ambitious 'ruinous project' failed in the north because the land was unsuitable but succeeded on one holding in the south. Thirteen farms became vacant. Loudon's more enduring impact, at the landlords expense, was on the landscape of the northern part of the estate where the Lodge Ponds were created to provide power to the new threshing mill. Fields were drained, hedges were grubbed up leaving larger trees standing and trees planted particularly on Cow Hill and along new roads in accordance with the projected plan. At times in 1809-1810 as many as 132 men were working on improvements.

1815 Stratton sold out for twice the asking price of 1807.

1815-1816 M. R. Boulton bought the farmland of Great Tew amounting to 2800 acres excluding the village and the closes as 14 farms and a few small lots. Over three-quarters of the land was arable and much of the pasture land lay in the park and on Carters (later Park) farm.

1815 Although much of the Manor House was demolished in 1803 parts evidently remained. The new Manor House was built nearer the village.

1815 The southern mill ceased working and was abandoned in the 1830's and in 1841 occupied by a farm labourer.

1816-1899 The earlier eviction of local farmers was only temporary and several of the chief farms were held for much of the 19th century by long established local families such as the Barlows at Park Farm (earlier Carters), the Nevilles at Court Farm and the Kimbers at Tracy Farm.

1816-1844 The rebuilding of Great Tew by M.R.Boulton (who seems hardly to have lived at Tew) in a very 'ornamental and singular style' occurred in the first phase between 1816-1818 when the bulk of the expenditure was on the mansion house and some of the principal farms notably Tracy, Beaconsfield and probably Park Farm. Boulton engaged the architect Thomas Rickman in 1820, later in 1828 Thomas Fulljames and later still Walter of Gloucester. During the first phase it seems likely that former outbuildings were converted and gaps between cottages infilled to form rows. The building work was distinguished by the use of sawn timber for floors, coppice poles for roofs, stone mullioned windows, dripmoulds with large diamond stops, stone door-heads and elaborate stone porches. The planting of trees throughout the village was probably part of the Rickman or Boulton plan. In 1818, Boulton was authorised to close part of the eastern street and Floods Lane and to provide a new straight link between The Square and The Green. The link road eventually provided was not on the agreed line and the eastern lane seems to have been closed by being absorbed into the Wilderness park by 1833.

1817 The Courts leet and baron met at the Horse and Groom (probably later the Falkland Arms)

by 1823 Loudon's farm had gone and been replaced by the nearby Cottenham Farm. His house probably went soon afterwards leaving just the threshing mill which was used for crushing bone in the 1830's and fell into disuse in 1881.

1827-1828 The Church and Chancel was restored by Thomas Rickman as was the vicarage.

1828 Two people were killed by lightning on Tracey's farm

1830's Employment again became a problem and in 1836 the parish became part of the Chipping Norton poor law union.

1834 The Gothic library was added to the Manor House.

1840 Boulton was asked to weigh the respective merits of stone slate and expensively insured thatch and chose the latter.

1841 The craftsmen and tradesmen included 3 smiths, 3 tailors, 3 carpenters, 2 sawyers, 2 grocers, 2 butchers, 2 bakers, 2 masons, a painter, a carrier, and a publican.

1842 M. R. Boulton died and was succeeded by his son M.P.W.Boulton who died in 1894 and grandson M.E.Boulton who died unmarried in 1914.

1845-1855 Congregations of 120 to 150 were recorded at the Church.

1847 The vestry organised a voluntary subscription to assist large families.

1850's The village Court with jury met to appoint constables, tithingmen, fieldmen and haywards and made orders for the management of open fields. The income for constables came from levies on yardland and 'townland' lost at inclosure. Although the village stocks were present during the period their use in England goes back to Anglo-Saxon times. (The pillory was abolished in England in 1837 and stocks were supposed to have fallen out of use before then).

1850-1856 The second phase of rebuilding included No. 31 (opposite the garden of Tulip Tree cottage), the school of 1851, two pairs of 'pattern book' cottages with gabled dormers and lattice windows on the main road west of Court Farm, buildings in the Crimea Yard of 1856 (dominated by the tall chimney of the saw-mills engine house which once contained a beam engine), a brickyard and presumably the pug-mill on the Hookerswell estate. The stone and wooden structure comprising a row of low gothic arches standing in the garden of Nos. 36 and 37(opposite Park Farm) apparently built to house beehives(near a site known in 1767 as the Dog Kennel) also dates from that time.

1854 There were 40 boys and 40 girls attending the new school. By 1867 95 pupils were being taught. The vicar reported that a third of the villagers were Baptists or Ranters.

1855 From that year the village was to take on its present day shape as a result of road closures which divided the village into 3 or 4 apparently unrelated groups of cottages. The main street (Old Road to The Green) which ran up to the Manor House was cut off by the new Park boundary (as well as the branch road to The Square and the track Floods Lane named after the Fludd family around 1560's) and the New Road was created west of the Manor House to The Lane by The Green. At the time there were several cottages on

Built 1675-1696

Left: Tulip Tree Cottage

the west side of the branch road.

1856 The new space west of the Manor House allowed a Tudor extension to be built by Fulljames and Walter.

1857 Little Tew became a separate parish although, since the mid 17th century, it had collected its own rates and also had its own constable, churchwarden, and overseer appointed by the Great Tew vestry.

1861 There had been some amalgamation of farms in the 19th century the principal ones were Park, Cottenham, Court, Ley in the north and in the south, Tracy, Beaconsfield and Hookerswell. The farms employed 76 men and 44 boys mostly on the southern arable farms and on Cottenham Farm in the north.

1868-1872 There was heavy expenditure at Tew Park when additions included the large kitchen garden south of the Ledwell Road.

1869 It was estimated that 150 Primitive Methodists were attending meetings in a cottage in the village.

1871 The building trades became more prominent with 7 masons and 4 carpenters, a painter, a stonelayer, a brickmaker, a bricklayer, a smith, a butcher and a combined grocers, butchers, and bakers shop employing 4 assistants.

1877 The turnpike at the end of Mill Lane by Banbury Hill was abolished. About the same time Great Tew was described as 'one of the best farmed parishes in the Midland counties'.

1890 Attendance at the school declined to 64 pupils.

1891 The number of houses had risen during the century to reach 102.

1894 A parish council was formed when Great Tew became part of Chipping Norton rural council.

1900-1960 During the period farming on the estate seems to have declined.

1901 The population of the village fell to 334.

1911 The proportion of permanent grass increased from a third in 1869 to nearly a half with a tenth under rotation.

1914 The unmarried owner M.E. Boulton died and the estate was administered by the Public Trustee allowing the deceased's sisters Clara Gertrude (died 1958) and Margaret having successive life interests. Long years in the hands of the Trustees saw a decline in the fortunes of the estate. The land was under-exploited, the farm buildings sometimes neglected or abandoned, the population diminished and vacant cottages fell into decay. For fifty years Great Tew experienced few of the physical and social changes that had transformed other villages.

1936 The school was reorganised for juniors and infants with an attendance of 31 including Little Tew pupils.

1939 There were 3 shops, The Post Office, The Butchers and The Haberdashers.

1939-1945 The second world saw the accidental destruction by fire of The Haberdashers shop on 5th November 1940 and later the wooden village hall in The Lane. The American forces (G.I.'s) occupied Cow Hill and the surrounding districts with their jeeps, half-tracks and tanks for almost a year from late in 1942 until their departure for the North African operation 'Torch'. There was much activity at the wartime bomber base at Enstone and one aircraft crashed in the field along Norton Road. The Manor House was used to board the orphans and handicapped children from bombing raids on Croydon supported in their domestic needs by many of the villagers and new residents escaping the war.

1945 The new buildings on Butchers Hill for a council estate were built and electricity came to a part of the village for the first time.

1951 The population fell to 204.

1960-1969 There was a recovery in farming with several farms kept in hand which remained mixed producing grain crops, sheep and cattle. The contrast between the arable south and pastoral north continued. A small sewerage plant was built by Coles's Brook below Cow Hill to which half the houses were connected. Piped water was also brought to the older houses.

1962 Major Eustace Robb, grandson of M.P.W.Boulton's sister Mary Ann, inherited the estate but had been living in the Manor House since 1952. The declared policy was to revive agricultural prosperity and to restore village properties for families employed locally thus preserving 'a rural community of rural workers'. The unusual social structure of Great Tew, the absence of commuters, week-enders or a 'retired professional element', aroused comment as early as the 1950's but many cottages became derelict under the policy.

1970 The Local Authority began to question the nature and timing of the estate policy. Thereafter Great Tew became the subject of local and national controversy in which many of the major issues of rural planning were raised.

1971 The population numbered 211.

1978 The village was declared a Conservation Area.

1979 There were 43 children on the school register.

1979 The parishioners opposed a plan to sell the vicarage house.

1980's Many cottages in the village remained derelict and ownership was granted to outsiders for the first time who by their personal and financial application sought to restore the cottages and gardens to their former ornamental appeal.